T0311749

Managing Your Academic Career

The definitive resource for mid-career professionals in the academy, this book provides a step-by-step guide to re-imagining the mid-career stage, regardless of career goals, whether aiming for full professorship or an administrative path, drawing on higher education, organizational studies, and human resource fields.

Essential guidance for scholars of faculty work, faculty developers, mid-career faculty members, and institutional leaders to build a strong foundation to design a diversified portfolio of mid-career stage programming is assured. The stories, examples, literature, and resources shared throughout this comprehensive work will provide inspiration, and reality checks, to mid-career faculty and the individuals charged with better supporting them. Readers will be able to:

- Identify their career (or departmental/institutional) goals and next steps
- Determine the gaps in needed skills, tools, and experiences to support goal achievement as next steps are pursued
- Manage the process of taking newfound skills, tools, strategies, and resources to arrive at the intended destination.

Higher education faculty, administrators, and other academic leaders will be empowered to take control of the mid-career stage by using the resources, strategies, and tools offered throughout the book to build, implement, and assess a robust mid-career faculty development program.

Vicki L. Baker, recognized as a 2020–2021 "Top 100 Visionary" in Education by the Global Forum for Education and Learning, stands at the forefront of innovation and strategy in faculty and leadership development. The author of *Charting Your Path to Full: A Guide for Women Associate Professors*, the lead author of *Developing Faculty in Liberal Arts Colleges*, and the lead editor of *Success After Tenure: Supporting Mid-Career Faculty*, Vicki has written over 85 peer-reviewed journal articles, book chapters, and invited opinion pieces on the topics of faculty and leadership development and higher education. She is the E. Maynard Aris Endowed Professor in Economics and Management at Albion College and the Director of the Albion College Community Collaborative (AC3). She earned her PhD (Higher Education) and MS (Management & Organization) from Penn State University, MBA from Clarion University, and BS from Indiana University of Pennsylvania.

"This guide provides clear, easy-to-use strategies and tools for mid-career faculty to reflect, course correct and reengage in their careers. It also provides a framework for administrators and academic leaders to build much needed mid-career faculty development programs at their own institutions."

Susan M. Drange, PhD, *Associate Vice Provost, Office of Faculty Development, Diversity and Engagement, Stanford University*

"*Managing Your Academic Career* is the definitive resource for mid-career faculty and administrators navigating the mid-career stage in pursuit of professional and personal fulfillment. Using a *bricoleur* approach, the book aptly addresses the individualized goals and aspirations of mid-career faculty and those tasked with supporting them, using case studies and reflective activities to create actionable plans."

Candace Hastings, PhD, *Director, Office of Faculty Development, Texas State University*

"Vicki Baker brings scholarship and consultation expertise to examine midcareer faculty (MCF)—a season of academic life full of potential but without time boundaries and mentoring of pre-tenure. Real issues coupled with research grounding, reflective activities, and practical strategies make this a must read for MCF and academic leaders."

Marilyn J. Amey, *Interim Associate Provost for Faculty and Academic Staff Development, Mildred B. Erickson Endowed Chair Emerita Professor of Higher, Adult, and Lifelong Education Department of Educational Administration, Michigan State University*

Managing Your Academic Career

A Guide to Re-Envision Mid-Career

Vicki L. Baker

Routledge
Taylor & Francis Group

NEW YORK AND LONDON

Cover image: © Lainey Yehl

First published 2022
by Routledge
605 Third Avenue, New York, NY 10158

and by Routledge
4 Park Square, Milton Park, Abingdon, Oxon, OX14 4RN

Routledge is an imprint of the Taylor & Francis Group, an informa business

Library of Congress Cataloging-in-Publication Data
Names: Baker, Vicki L., 1978– author.
Title: Managing your academic career : a guide to re-envision mid-career / Vicki L. Baker.
Description: New York, NY : Routledge, 2022. |
Includes bibliographical references and index.
Identifiers: LCCN 2021055996 | ISBN 9781032062402 (hardback) |
ISBN 9781032062396 (paperback) | ISBN 9781003201311 (ebook)
Subjects: LCSH: College teachers–Vocational guidance–United States. |
College teachers–Employment–United States. | College administrators–
Vocational guidance–United States. | College administrators–Employment–
United States. | Mid-career–United States.
Classification: LCC LB1778.2 .B36 2022 |
DDC 378.1/20230973–dc23/eng/20220110
LC record available at https://lccn.loc.gov/2021055996

ISBN: 9781032062402 (hbk)
ISBN: 9781032062396 (pbk)
ISBN: 9781003201311 (ebk)

DOI: 10.4324/9781003201311

Typeset in Sabon
by Newgen Publishing UK

To McKenna and Henley my favorite humans on the planet

Contents

Figure

Tables

Foreword

Dr. Kimberly Griffin
Professor, Associate Dean of Graduate Studies & Faculty Affairs
University of Maryland

There are times when I read books, and I am a passive observer. Perhaps there is a skill that I am trying to build or develop, or something that I am trying to understand. I can keep the text at arm's length, engaging it from a purely scholarly perspective. *Managing Your Academic Career: A Guide to Re-envision Mid-Career* was not that kind of read for me. Vicki Baker's outstanding text immediately drew me in. It certainly engaged me as a scholar who seeks to better understand career development, mentoring, and efforts to promote equity in the academy. But I could not ignore how this text called not only to what I study, but also so many parts of who I am: The recently promoted full professor, the Black cis-gendered woman, the mom of an active and fun-loving toddler, and the associate dean charged with faculty affairs and development.

Before I finished the first chapter, one of my favorite quotes from Audre Lorde (2020) pushed its way from the back to the front of my mind: "If I didn't define myself for myself, I would be crunched into other people's fantasies for me and eaten alive" (p. 129) Making sense of career development and progression was somehow easier for me early in my career. The work was challenging and I was often uncertain, but figuring out who I was and what I wanted was embedded in my graduate training and early years as a professor. When students enter graduate school, they are socialized into the norms of their discipline and learn directly and indirectly what it means to be in the academy. There are a series of guidelines to follow and degree requirements to complete that allow people to not only earn a PhD, but also develop an academic identity and content expertise (Austin, 2002; Austin & McDaniels, 2006; Griffin et al., 2020). If those with a PhD enter a tenure-track academic role, there is a timeline and a specific goal to reach. While the guidelines may not be clearly communicated and many early career scholars feel unprepared to take on faculty work (Austin et al., 2007; Eddy & Gaston-Gayles, 2008), there is a general level of awareness among administrators and leaders that faculty need to be supported and need to define themselves and their agendas to be successful (Gonzalez et al., 2019).

But Baker's book reminds us of what may feel obvious; the support, the intentionality, and specific goal with a timeline goes away post tenure. Informally, associate professors are encouraged to step into their authentic selves as academics without the worries of whether they will be viewed favorably by their colleagues. But what does that mean and look like? How does one re-think and re-establish oneself, particularly given that students, colleagues, administrators, and institutional leaders are eager to rush in with new demands and obligations (Baldwin et al., 2005; Gardner & Blackstone, 2013)? And while I remember feeling like I had done a pretty good job of defining myself and what I did, it became increasingly important to clarify what I *did not do* in my post-tenure years. Other people's fantasies and ideas about the scholar I was and what I could do loomed large. In many ways, I was left on my own to determine what I would and would not do moving forward based on an unclear sense of what would be required if I wanted to be promoted to full professor, and where I wanted my career to go next.

This book, at its core, is about empowering individuals to define themselves, intentionally charting a path toward goals that align with their values and commitments. We often think of faculty careers as being highly autonomous. You do not really have a "boss" or well-defined work hours. Academic freedom is celebrated as a foundational value of the profession. And tenure makes termination very unlikely. While these conditions may sound ideal, research shows that the lack of structure and clearly defined responsibilities can often make academic careers more challenging to manage (Berg & Seeber, 2018; Gappa & Austin, 2010). Working anytime can easily (and often does) become working all the time. In the face of increasing asks and demands, faculty are expected to take personal responsibility and "protect their time." There are few institutional structures to ensure that workloads are distributed equitably, despite well-documented disparities in who gets asked to engage in labor that is often invisible and unrewarded (Misra et al., 2021; O'Meara et al., 2018). And there are few intentional, structured opportunities for faculty to reflect on their purpose, their values, and their goals, both generally and directly in relation to what they are doing from day to day.

Without a sense of our values and purpose in the academy, goals aligned with those values, or information and support to intentionally pursue those goals, mid-career faculty are vulnerable to aimlessness, dissatisfaction, and languishing. Our mid-career colleagues are at risk of being defined as something they had no intention of being. They are eaten alive, working perpetually but aimlessly with no respite in sight.

Baker's book is an intervention, in many ways designed for faculty to interrupt the cycle of dissatisfaction and malaise endemic to mid-career faculty. This text embraces the notion that mid-career faculty have agency and can, indeed, define themselves. Agency is not the same as assuming one has complete control; an agentic perspective acknowledges that there are barriers and external factors that can have an impact on their life and outcomes (Archer, 2000). I am particularly grateful for how this book calls attention to how identity-based oppression manifests in the academy, creating uniquely threatening experiences that challenge the advancement of minoritized scholars. As a Black cis-gendered woman, descriptions of the experiences of faculty of color, women, and specific attention to women of color were resonant and appreciated. Understanding systemic dynamics creates an opportunity for the development of agency, reflected in strategic thinking and behaviors that allow individuals to leverage support and resources to navigate challenges as they arise and make informed choices whenever possible (O'Meara, 2015; O'Meara & Campbell, 2011).

This book serves as such an important tool in fostering the agency of mid-career faculty. It expertly integrates narrative, research, exercises, and concrete guidance, all while helping mid-career faculty better understand the complex contexts they work within and how to ask the right questions of themselves and others to make decisions and move forward. The case studies woven through each chapter were particularly useful and felt familiar and relatable. Sometimes it is easier to understand and see a problem when framed in the context of someone else's experience. As academics we are rarely vulnerable enough with each other to have the opportunity to benefit from our shared insecurities, questions, and mistakes. This text creates a new opportunity for learning through its transparency and candor that I am sure will benefit many trying to chart their next best step forward.

While this text certainly has great value for mid-career faculty to help themselves and make meaning of their careers, I also read this book through the lens of my administrative work, thinking about how this text can be used as a tool and guide for mentors and academic leaders. Baker's work is an important reminder that mid-career faculty often lack and are in critical need of mentorship and guidance; however, what can and should take place within the context of those relationships is ill-defined and both access to and the quality of experience within faculty mentoring relationships are inconsistent at best (Johnson, 2015). This work offers important guidance and training for those who will be working directly with mid-career faculty, providing a framework for the questions they can and should be asking and the forms of support they can provide. Importantly, I think that this text can make mentors more attuned to the wide variety of needs and challenges mid-career faculty face, making them more sensitive to potential differences and similarities based on discipline and identity. I hope mentors come away from this text with the capacity to be better listeners and more aware of barriers and the unique ways they manifest for scholars who are facing structural oppression and inequality.

It is tempting to assign primary value of this text to mid-career faculty and their mentors, focusing our efforts on supporting individuals as they navigate their campuses. However, it has become clear to me as a scholar and campus administrator that real change and equitable opportunity for thriving and advancement in the academy are dependent on leaders' ability to change policies, practices, and perhaps most importantly, culture. In so many cases, faculty face problems that are structural and systemic. Unequal workloads, lack of appreciation of service and emotional work, and inconsistent support feel like individual problems, but Baker's book highlights how these issues become barriers for all. Such issues reproduce inequity in the academy because of how they become embedded in academic culture, disciplinary norms, and evaluation and promotion processes. Thus, in addition to being a critical tool in efforts to support mid-career faculty as individuals, this text leaves leaders with crucial questions to ask themselves about how to ensure that all faculty have opportunities to thrive. Some of this work is rooted in more intentional and widespread programmatic efforts to engage in the process of self-definition. However, this book is another reminder that leaders must do the work of addressing the ways that our current structures, systems, and norms perpetuate inequality. National conversations about recruitment and hiring of faculty and tenure and promotion, focusing particularly on how they are marked by sexism, racism, and heterosexism are critical; however, this book adds to the growing chorus demanding that we address marginalization beyond hiring and tenure, addressing the long-term implications of these dynamics on faculty retention and satisfaction.

References

Archer, M. S. (2000). *Being human: The problem of agency*. Cambridge University Press.

Austin, A. E. (2002). Preparing the next generation of faculty: Graduate school as socialization to the academic career. *The Journal of Higher Education, 73*(1), 94–122.

Austin, A. E., & McDaniels, M. (2006). Preparing the professoriate of the future: Graduate student socialization for faculty roles. In J. C. Smart (Ed.), *Higher education: Handbook for theory and research* (pp. 397–456). Springer, Dordrecht.

Austin, A. E., Sorcinelli, M. D., & McDaniels, M. (2007). Understanding new faculty background, aspirations, challenges, and growth. In R. P. Perry & J. C. Smart (Eds.), *The scholarship of teaching and learning in higher education: An evidence-based perspective* (pp. 39–89). Springer, Dordrecht.

Baldwin, R. G., Lunceford, C. J., & Vanderlinden, K. E. (2005). Faculty in the middle years: Illuminating an overlooked phase of academic life. *The Review of Higher Education*, *29*(1), 97–118.

Berg, M., & Seeber, B. K. (2018). *The slow professor*. University of Toronto Press.

Eddy, P. L., & Gaston-Gayles, J. L. (2008). New faculty on the block: Issues of stress and support. *Journal of Human Behavior in the Social Environment*, *17*(1–2), 89–106.

Gappa, J. M., & Austin, A. E. (2010). Rethinking academic traditions for twenty-first-century faculty. *AAUP Journal of Academic Freedom*, *1*(1), 1–20.

Gardner, S. K., & Blackstone, A. (2013). "Putting in your time": Faculty experiences in the process of promotion to professor. *Innovative Higher Education*, *38*(5), 411–425.

Gonzalez, L. M., Wester, K. L., & Borders, L. D. (2019). Supports and barriers to new faculty researcher development. *Studies in Graduate and Postdoctoral Education*, *10*(1), 21–34.

Griffin, K. A., Baker, V. L., & O'Meara, K. (2020). Doing, caring, and being: "Good" mentoring and its role in the socialization of graduate students of color in STEM. In J. C. Weidman & L. DeAngelo (Eds.), *Socialization in Higher Education and the Early Career* (pp. 223–239). Springer, Cham.

Johnson, W. B. (2015). *On being a mentor: A guide for higher education faculty*. Routledge. www.taylorfrancis.com/books/mono/10.4324/9781315669120/being-mentor-brad-johnson

Lorde, A. (2020). *The selected works of Audre Lorde*. WW Norton & Company.

Misra, J., Kuvaeva, A., O'meara, K., Culpepper, D. K., & Jaeger, A. (2021). Gendered and racialized perceptions of faculty workloads. *Gender & Society*, *35*(3), 358–394.

O'Meara, K. (2015). A career with a view: Agentic perspectives of women faculty. *The Journal of Higher Education*, *86*(3), 331–359.

O'Meara, K., & Campbell, C. M. (2011). Faculty sense of agency in decisions about work and family. *The Review of Higher Education*, *34*(3), 447–476.

O'Meara, K., Jaeger, A., Misra, J., Lennartz, C., & Kuvaeva, A. (2018). Undoing disparities in faculty workloads: A randomized trial experiment. *PloS one*, *13*(12), e0207316. https://journals.plos.org/plosone/article?id=10.1371/journal.pone.0207316

Acknowledgments

As I progress along my career journey, there have been so many people along the way who offer support and encouragement. First, I want to thank all my clients and the institutions who have sought my coaching and guidance as they advance along their careers and seek to support their faculty and administrators. Your stories fill this book; without you, this book does not exist.

Second, thanks to several key women in my personal and professional sphere. To my dear friend and collaborator Laura Lunsford who I shared the idea for this book with and who facilitated an introduction with Meredith Norwich, my wonderful editor at Routledge. Your support and positivity are so greatly appreciated. Big shout out to my amazing copyeditor, Sarah Ashlock, who has worked with me on every major project to date and is a miracle worker. Lainey Yehl a super talented freelance graphic designer who took my content and brought it to life visually for my related keynote addresses and workshops inspired by the content from this book. Lastly, my dear friend Kim Griffin who graciously agreed to write the Foreword to this book. Thank you all so much!!!

Finally, to my family who is my foundation. I wrote this book during the pandemic because I was inspired to help other faculty and campus leaders navigate the strangest of times in the academy. My kids, McKenna and Henley, you inspire me every day, and I am so grateful to be your mother. Thank you to my husband Bryan, who supports my dreams and has helped create this beautiful life we have built together. Finally, we would be lost without my mother, Mary Ann, who helped us manage this academic year with virtual schooling and in person work. Not a day goes by where I do not feel a profound sense of gratitude to pursue a career for which I am deeply passionate about.

About the Author

Recognized as a "Top 100 Visionary" in Education by the Global Forum for Education and Learning (2020–2021), you will find Vicki at the forefront of innovation and strategy in faculty and leadership development. As a faculty member herself and Fulbright Specialist Alumna her goal is to help faculty members and colleges and universities thrive.

Vicki is the author of *Charting Your Path to Full: A Guide for Women Associate Professors*, lead editor of *Success After Tenure: Supporting Mid-Career Faculty*, and lead co-author of *Developing Faculty in Liberal Arts Colleges*. Her forthcoming book, *Managing Your Academic Career: A Guide to Re-envision Mid-Career* (Routledge/Taylor & Francis) will be in print in spring, 2022. In addition, she has written over 85 peer-reviewed journal articles, book chapters, invited opinion pieces for higher education news media outlets, case studies, and blogs on the topics of faculty and leadership development and higher education. She earned her PhD (Higher Education) and MS (Management & Organization) from Penn State University, MBA from Clarion University, and BS from Indiana University of Pennsylvania. She is a professor, economics and management, at Albion College and an instructor for Penn State University's World Campus. Prior to joining the academy as a faculty member, Vicki worked at Harvard Business School (Executive Education) and AK Steel Corporation.

Vicki's work has been featured in national and international media outlets including *WalletHub*, *Times Higher Education*, *Hechinger Report*, *Wall Street Journal*, *The Atlantic*, *USA Today*, *New York Times*, *Chronicle of Higher Education*, and the *Huffington Post*. She regularly consults with industry and higher education institutions on the topics of leadership, faculty development, change management, and mentoring.

Vicki has conducted workshops, scholarly presentations, and keynote addresses at professional associations including the Association for the Study of Higher Education, the Council for the Advancement of Higher Education Programs, the American Educational Research Association, and the Professional and Organizational Development Network in Higher Education (POD). Her teaching and scholarship have garnered attention within and outside of her institution. She has been recognized as the Arthur Anderson Teacher of the Year, Phi Beta Kappa Scholar of the Year, Student's Choice "Professor of the Year," Arthur Anderson New Teacher of the Year, Most Valuable Professor, and "Professor of the Day" by the Michigan Colleges Alliance (MCA). Vicki was also a "Best Article Award 2012" Top 3 Finalist—*Personnel Psychology* and Highly Commended Winner for Excellence from the Emerald Literati Network (*Journal of Managerial Psychology*). Her work has been funded by the Luce Foundation and the National Science Foundation.

Vicki enjoys spending time with her husband, two children, and their dog. She participates in interval training three days a week and is an avid reader.

Introduction

> I don't even know where to begin. I've had this laser focus for so long, that I feel a bit lost, lacking the mental energy to take that first step.

This is a line from an email I received from a faculty member seeking help to navigate her next season of life—mid-career. The sentiments shared here are familiar to me as an academic myself, and are likely to sound familiar for other mid-career faculty (MCF) and the academic leaders tasked with supporting them. For many, earning promotion and tenure (P&T) is that all-important brass ring. However, the other side of this momentous occasion fails to be the utopia most academics imagine.

I am someone who followed the very traditional professorial path. I entered my doctoral program at Penn State with aspirations of becoming a faculty member. I was fortunate to earn an instructor position during my doctoral experience in the Smeal College of Business teaching undergraduate courses in management, organizational behavior, and human resources. It was in this role that I discovered my love of teaching undergraduate business while also engaging in scholarship about doctoral student identity development. I was curious to know what, and who, contributed to the success of doctoral students and the process by which they developed a professional identity as future business academics. My interests in mentoring, professional development, and supporting others' career advancement were born.

Fast forward to today and I am an endowed full professor at Albion College, a liberal arts college in Albion, Michigan. I often describe it as the Norman Rockwell of liberal arts colleges—it is the quintessential liberal arts college campus you would expect, no matter the direction from which you view it. I am *the* management professor in the Department of Economics and Management (and only one on campus). My students affectionately refer to me as "The 'M' in E&M" given my disciplinary responsibilities on campus. I live near two major research universities

DOI: 10.4324/9781003201311-1

where I have been an adjunct professor, served on doctoral dissertation committees, held leadership positions on research grants, and collaborated with faculty members. My geographical proximity to inspiring institutions of higher education has allowed me to merge my passions for teaching undergraduate business and pursuing scholarship and practice that focuses on the faculty experience. Throughout my research and practice, a consistent observation has emerged regardless of institution type: Faculty members, particularly at mid-career, need and seek support and opportunities to guide their professional (and personal) evolution, and campus leaders tasked with supporting them seek guidance and resources.

I earned full professorship six years ago at the age of 38, with significant career runway still ahead. While I certainly celebrated the accomplishment, it felt a little hollow; there was no more distinct career milestone to work toward and no resources to help me think through what that meant or, more importantly, how I could create my own. Throughout my interactions with faculty members within and outside my own institution, it has become very apparent that I am not alone in those feelings and needs.

Strength in Numbers

My scholarly agenda and professorial career have afforded me many opportunities to interact with and support faculty members across the United States and also internationally as a Fulbright Specialist in the Netherlands. I am in awe of these faculty members, spanning the ways they contribute to their institutions and departments, engage with their communities, and maintain an unyielding passion for their students. To say these interactions are inspirational would be a bit of an understatement. I would be remiss if I did not acknowledge the privilege that accompanies this career; I must also admit that a great deal of commitment and sacrifice are close companions.

Throughout these opportunities, I have found comfort in knowing I am not alone in my experiences, concerns, and aspirations for a fulfilling career. A career that brings with it opportunities to reimagine oneself as a professional, where I can take risks and contribute in meaningful ways to the stakeholders I hold most dear. The need for a life "outside of the academy" is also present, and even more so as we in higher education grapple with a global pandemic, which will reverberate throughout the academy for years, and perhaps decades, to come. The present is an appropriate time to reflect on priorities and expectations bestowed upon us by ourselves and others as we ponder the not so simple question: What's next? It is a question I have been asked by more MCF and campus leaders throughout my consulting work than I can count, and it motivated me to write this book.

Mid-Career: Then and Now

Recently, a colleague and I completed a meta-synthesis of four decades of research and practice about MCF (Baker & Manning, 2021). During this intensive review of the literature, predominant themes emerged that help situate mid-career in the broader context of the academy and professorial career. Efforts by scholars and practitioners dedicated to this population of faculty laid the needed foundation to contribute to current understanding and knowledge about mid-career, a more nebulous stage of career and life compared to other phases accompanied by clear milestones. I briefly discuss a few of those themes as important grounding to the aims of this book and the content featured in it.

First, recognition for the need to increase faculty morale and create varying career paths within the professoriate at mid-career is not new to the academy. In fact, literature dating back to the late 1970s (see, e.g., Golembiewski, 1978) and 1980s (see, e.g., Baldwin, 1981; Baldwin & Blackburn, 1981) revealed that MCF, especially women and faculty of color, were particularly vulnerable to feelings of stagnation. Scholars noted many MCF lacked career direction (Ward & Wolf-Wendel, 2016), while also recognizing that institutional structures, or lack thereof, were contributing factors to MCF being under supported as compared to their early career peers (Belker, 1985; Petter et al., 2018). Fueling these feelings was the tension between research and teaching and the additional administrative and leadership responsibilities that were bestowed upon MCF (Berheide, 1986; Sorcinelli, 1985), a professional reality that still resonates today (Ross, 2015).

Second, is the recognition that the faculty career is multifaceted, requiring a diversity of supports to traverse this phase of career and life successfully (Rice, 1984, 1986). In fact, this research stream introduced the career stage model and emphasized the unique aspects of mid-career including the challenges faced by faculty in this season of their lives (Balwin & Blackburn, 1981). Calls for a more interdisciplinary approach to understanding, studying, and supporting the professoriate were shared by scholars including Rice (1984). This approach resulted in the recognition of and appreciation for the differences present in the academy among faculty beyond discipline and required more clearly defined strategies to provide needed developmental support.

Third, scholars and practitioners highlighted the importance of the mid-career stage to MCF members as they advance in the academy and to the institutions that employ them (Blain, 2020). As a population, MCF have the ability to leverage their collective power due to their institutional and disciplinary knowledge. Innovation, creativity, and leadership can be harnessed from this population of faculty given the amount of career runway remaining. Simply stated, MCF *are* the next generation of institutional leaders (Baker et al., 2019), poised to assume this responsibility *if* they are enabled to do so.

The review of four decades of research and practice shows a very clear awareness about the potential of MCF at the individual and institutional levels (Baker & Manning, 2021) and reveals a collective agreement about the importance of investing in this population of faculty. I am pleased to see more recent targeted efforts geared toward MCF such as the Mid-Career Faculty Workshop sponsored by the Council for the Advancement of Higher Education Programs through the Association for the Study of Higher Education and the varied resources highlighted in "From Associate to Full Professor" published by Inside Higher Ed (Blain, 2020). Yet, compared to early-career faculty, MCF infrastructure and programming are woefully behind. MCF and the institutional leaders charged with supporting them need guidance.

Positionality

The MCF I have the great fortune to engage with as part of my scholarship and practice inspire me, and it is their experiences and needs that compelled me to write this book. The chapters are informed by my consulting experience in faculty and leadership development, scholarship focused on the professoriate, and disciplinary insights from higher education, organizational studies, and human resources. I know and appreciate the importance of my positionality as it shapes and influences the issues presented and the tools, strategies, and resources offered throughout. To that end, I share my positionality in this section.

I have been an academic for nearly 20 years having spent time at both research universities and liberal arts colleges, predominantly. I am a White woman full professor in the male-dominated fields of business and higher education. My teaching load is a 3–3, and the courses I teach span leadership, management, organizational studies, and human resource management. I also currently hold a leadership position on my campus (director-level) for a new initiative focused on building an experiential learning lab that connects student teams and community partners in a consultative capacity. I am tasked with building this program from the ground up, rooted in the values and mission of my institution. I have a one-hour commute to work, one way.

I research the faculty trajectory, focused predominantly at mid-career (prior to I focused on early career faculty experiences). That work has spanned institution types and faculty populations. Most recently, I focused my attention toward the experiences of women faculty at mid-career, including women of color (Baker, 2020) by highlighting their experiences in the academy and offering resources to help advance in their careers, in spite of existing barriers and challenges.

Finally, and most important to me, I am a married mother of two elementary-aged children who are 19 months apart; I have primary financial responsibility for my family and household, as well as primary responsibility for childcare. My husband is a golf professional and general manager of a university-run golf facility and golf courses, and during golf season (8–9 months pending Michigan weather), he works 80–100 hours a week, including evenings and weekends.

It is these roles, identities, experiences, and perspectives that inform my interpretation of the problems presented and solutions offered.

Purpose of the Book

I recently had a conversation about faculty development needs with a dean of faculty at a liberal arts college. Upon review of their institutional faculty development offerings, we acknowledged the lack of comprehensive and long-term mentoring available to faculty members beyond their first year of employment. As we brainstormed ideas, the dean simply stated, "Department chairs need to mentor their faculty and to be better mentors. I plan to email them to communicate this expectation." While I agreed with that observation, I replied by asking, "What support do you provide to department chairs to help them meet this expectation?" My question was met with silence.

This brief exchange epitomizes the core of the problem—MCF need mentorship, which is lacking in most institutional contexts; those tasked with supporting them need mentorship and guidance, which too is lacking or inadequate in most institutional contexts. Despite the strides made and attention paid to the mid-career stage, there is still a lack of step-by-step guidance for faculty and institutional leaders. This book answers that need. Three aims guide the organization of this book to help faculty and campus leaders:

- Identify their career (or departmental/institutional) goals and next steps.
- Determine the gaps in needed skills, tools, and experiences to support goal achievement as next steps are pursued.
- Manage the process of taking newfound skills, tools, strategies, and resources to arrive at the intended destination.

My goal is to create a singular resource in which both MCF *and* institutional leaders are served as they work independently and collaboratively to fulfill their professional and personal pursuits. I want individuals to feel supported, and my aim in writing this book is to provide that guidance along with relevant, accessible resources. Perhaps most important, I want MCF and institutional leaders to feel seen and validated; their concerns, challenges faced, and needs are real. Whatever the professional (or personal) goal, the needed tools, resources, and strategies are included in this book to achieve them.

Who Should Read This Book?

If you are a faculty member or campus leader in higher education, this book is for you and will be one of your go to professional resources as you seek to advance in your career and manage your professional roles and responsibilities. By reading this book, scholars and practitioners of faculty work, faculty developers, MCF members, and institutional leaders (e.g., department chair, dean of faculty) will receive needed guidance to build a strong foundation to design a diversified portfolio of mid-career stage programming. This book is the most comprehensive mid-career resource that offers individual faculty *and* departmental/institutional tools and strategies. The stories, examples, literature, and resources shared throughout this book provide inspiration and reality checks to MCF and the individuals charged with better supporting them.

How to Use it

Throughout my faculty development research and practice, consistent "problems" surfaced either from the MCF members' or institutional leaders' perspectives. Often times these problems are interrelated. Knowing the consistency with which these problems present themselves, I organized the book based on these problems with a single problem featured per chapter.

I illustrate a problem in an opening vignette or mini case study, followed by an explicit problem statement. I situate the problem in scholarship and practice, and then revisit the opening vignette or mini case to analyze the contributing factors and key stakeholders. Actionable solutions, tools, and strategies are offered along with additional recommendations and resources. A summary of the main ideas and next steps conclude each chapter. The organization of the book provides ultimate flexibility. Each chapter and its featured problem can serve as a stand-alone resource, or can be read either in the order presented or non-sequentially based on the targeted needs of the reader.

This book was written with the reader in mind—I wanted to create a resource in which the reader can "interact" with the book, take notes directly on pages, flag pages to return to, and walk away with tangible plans and tools. The shared activities are my go-to tools when serving as an academic coach and consultant to faculty and institutions. You will see working/writing sections embedded in each chapter, including guided question prompts and outlined action steps.

Chapter Overview/Organization of Book

The book is organized into three parts. In Part 1, "The Individual Faculty Perspective," Chapters 1–4 highlight critical challenges faced by MCF, including actionable solutions to address those challenges. Chapter 1 lays the groundwork for thinking through why and how MCF need to reimagine the next phase of their careers. Chapter 2 provides guidance on how to plan for the next phase and walks the readers through various goal-setting and problem-solving strategies and tools. Chapter 3 helps MCF locate and turn P&T language and institutional strategic imperatives into a framework to organize professional advancement goals (e.g., the advancement to full professorship or an administrative career path). Finally, Chapter 4 offers concrete guidance on how to execute the developed short- and long-term plans.

In Part 2, "Departmental and Institutional Perspectives," Chapters 5–8 highlight the disconnect between institutional expectations and practice by offering assessment tools, recommendations on related training and development programming, and strategies for engaging in capacity-building to work toward the creation of a robust MCF portfolio of programs. Chapter 5 focuses on the department chair level and offers guidance on how to be an effective mentor to MCF. Chapter 6 continues the focus on the department chair and offers needed guidance to help these individuals advance their professional goals through mentorship while serving in this leadership role. Chapter 7 takes an institutional view and includes an assessment strategy to learn more about present faculty development offerings as a means of investing in a more robust faculty development portfolio. Chapter 8 continues the institutional focus and walks the reader through possible organizational and infrastructure adjustments and communication strategies regarding faculty development offerings.

In Part 3, "Thriving at Mid-Career," Chapter 9 serves as the conclusion of the book. Meta-themes are revisited along with targeted action steps organized by key stakeholder (e.g., MCF, faculty developers, and campus leaders). Additional recommendations are offered, such as ways to incorporate disciplinary and institutional considerations. See Table I.1 for a snapshot of the featured problems across these chapters to help inform a targeted reading strategy should that be of use.

This book is written in the first person, given I am wearing my academic coach/consulting hat as I write. I pursue this field because I am passionate about helping others advance in their careers, and it is my engagement in this work that fuels my own professional evolution. Feel free to reach out to let me know your thoughts and tell me how you used this book to support your own or your institutional reimagining processes. You can find me at my website www.leadmentordevelop.com.

Now let's get to work!

Table 1.1 Featured Chapter Problems

Chapter	Featured Problem
1	Lack of clearly defined career hurdles or developmental milestones
2	Limited dedicated resources and developmental programming aimed at mid-career
3	Inadequate guidance on how to advance toward professional (and personal) goals
4	No formal strategy; poorly articulated advancement plans
5	Disconnect between role expectations and available training and development to achieve such expectations
6	Role overload and limited access to mentors for support
7	Needs of seasoned faculty not met with existing faculty development programming
8	Faculty development programming not a focus of the existing institutional infrastructure

References

Baker, V. L., Lunsford, L. G., & Pifer, M. J. (2019). Patching up the "leaking leadership pipeline": Fostering mid-career faculty succession management. *Research in Higher Education, 60*(6), 823–843.

Baker, V. L. (2020). *Charting your path to full: A guide for women associate professors*. Rutgers University Press.

Baker, V. L., & Manning, C. E. (2021). A mid-career faculty agenda: A review of four decades of research and practice. *Higher Education: Handbook of Theory and Research: Volume 36*, 1–66.

Baldwin, R. G., (1981). *Expanding faculty options*. American Association for Higher Education.

Baldwin, R. G., & Blackburn, R. T. (1981). The academic career as a developmental process: Implications for higher education. *The Journal of Higher Education, 52*(6), 598–614.

Belker, J. S. (1985). The education of mid-career professors: Is it continuing? *College Teaching, 33*(2), 68–71.

Berheide, C. W. (1986). Discussion and commentary on the academic profession in transition. *Teaching Sociology, 14*(1), 35–39.

Blain, K. (May 22, 2020). From associate to full professor. *Inside Higher Ed*. www.insidehighered.com/advice/2020/05/22/guidance-how-move-associate-full-professor-opinion?utm_source=Inside%20Higher%20Ed&utm_campaign=15b7f9faf8-DNU_2019_COPY_02&utm_medium=email&utm_term=0_1fcbc04421-15b7f9faf8-197499405&mc_cid=15b7f9faf8&mc_eid=d7c23a94a2&fbclid=IwAR3zS_4WNsGkR6pEzyQQi4Ng8vRt8ANgkQkJStO2x8VFrjtaNf-ecWC584Y

Golembiewski, R. T. (1978). Mid-life transition and mid-career crisis: A special case for individual development. *Public Administration Review, 38*(3), 215–222.

Petter, S., Richardson, S., & Randolph, A. B. (2018). Stuck in the middle: Reflections from the AMCIS mid-career workshop. *Communications of the Association for Information Systems, 34*(1), 557–576.

Rice, R. E. (1984). Being professional academically. *To Improve the Academy, 5,* 5–13.

Rice, R. E. (1986). The academic profession in transition: Toward a new social fiction. *Teaching Sociology, 14*(1), 12–23.

Ross, C. (2015). Teaching renewal for mid-career faculty: Attending to the whole person. *To Improve the Academy, 34*(1–2), 270–289.

Sorcinelli, M. D. (1985). Faculty careers: Satisfactions and discontents. *To Improve the Academy, 4*(1), 44–62.

Ward, K., & Wolf-Wendel, L. (2016). Academic motherhood: Mid-career perspectives and the ideal worker norm. *New Directions for Higher Education, 2016*(176), 11–23.

Part I

The Individual Faculty Perspective

Chapter 1

Reimagining the Next Phase of Your Career

Sam, an associate professor in STEM, earned promotion and tenure two years ago at a comprehensive university. They "took a year off" from what they referred to as the hamster wheel that is the promotion and tenure pathway; the journey to get there was not without its challenges, personal and professional. Sam is an "out" LGBTQ faculty member on their campus but is still guarded given the campus is surrounded by rather conservative communities. Over the past two years, Sam went on sabbatical and was able to finish some lingering projects and felt good about having a "clean slate" from which to build. Now that Sam feels like they are in a better space mentally and emotionally, they are eager to advance toward full professorship. Sam reached out to trusted colleagues to have preliminary conversations about their experiences and plans (some had already earned full professorship and others had plans to do so in the near future). Sam realized, however, that their colleagues were successful despite of a lack of resources and developmental supports at their institution, rather than due to targeted programming to help faculty members advance towards full professorship. Sam quickly realized they needed to take matters into their own hands but struggled to envision what those could (or should) be beyond some basic preliminary steps. Sam also realized their faculty handbook language was unclear about the general promotion process and timeline. For example, Sam heard three different associate rank requirements one must be at before submitting materials; Sam is also not clear if faculty at their institution need to be nominated by their chair to advance to full professorship or if self-nominations are accepted, given the mixed responses they are hearing. Sam is beginning to wonder if advancing to full is worth it, especially given the lack of guidelines, developmental support, and mentoring.

DOI: 10.4324/9781003201311-3

Sam's experience is unfortunate, but sadly, not unusual in the academy. Extensive scholarship has featured mid-career faculty (MCF) facing similar experiences to Sam and shows that the underlying problem is a **lack of clearly defined career hurdles or developmental milestones**. As previously noted, the professorial path for those on the tenure track is prescribed starting as early as the doctoral student experience. Disciplinary nuances and institution type (e.g., research university, comprehensive college/university, liberal arts college, and community college) certainly contribute to the mid-career experience and how faculty members evolve as professionals. Regardless of discipline and institution type, however, aspiring faculty members in the academy seeking to advance in their careers traditionally: (a) earn their doctorates, (b) serve as post-doctoral fellows in some disciplinary fields, (c) seek to secure tenure-track positions, (d) serve as assistant professors for a clearly specified period of time (typically seven years where a tenure system is present), and (e) submit dossier materials for promotion and tenure (P&T) consideration. Once this P&T hurdle is surpassed, the prior structure and guidance is now lacking or non-existent.

This chapter focuses on the ill-defined mid-career stage and the associated implications of that reality. Later in the book (see Chapters 7 and 8), I offer an institutional perspective into this problem; here I share insights and knowledge from the individual faculty member perspective. This reality has serious implications for how faculty members experience and engage in the academy after achieving P&T. For many, those implications are negative and can have long-lasting consequences at the individual and institutional levels.

Lack of Clearly Defined Hurdles and Developmental Milestones—Why Should We Care?

Characterized as the "bridge between employee generations" (Baldwin & Chang, 2006), MCF are the backbone of higher education institutions. They serve as mentors and sources of support for early career colleagues while also serving as formal and informal leaders on their respective campuses (Baker et al., 2019). Their contribution is critical to the success and vitality of their institutions (Strage & Merdinger, 2015). Simply put, "Midcareer, tenured faculty members power their institutions" (Flaherty, 2017). Yet, they offer their support with little to no institutional resources to do so effectively. In fact, teaching, leadership, and service often do not "count" toward professional advancement within the academy, a reality that is consistent across institution types (Baker et al., 2019) and is disadvantageous for women and faculty of color given they traditionally spend more of their professional hours engaged in these areas (Perry, 2014; Strunk, 2020). While on the surface, I think most people would agree this is problematic; I also think this insight should prompt the question—Why should we care?

Mid-career professionals are the least satisfied employee population, a finding consistent in higher education and industry (Baker et al., 2017; Gibbons, 2018). This finding should cause concern for all of us, especially given MCF are *the* largest cohort of faculty in the academy (Grant-Vallone & Ensher, 2017), and institutions rely on and are in need of their contributions to support the overall functioning and advancement of the institutions in which they are employed.

According to research, being ill-prepared and under-supported at mid-career has individual and organizational implications:

- Less than 50% of decisions made in mid-career were rated as successful (Minsky & Peters, 2019).
- Longer time in rank, or "stalling," at certain career stages for women and other minorities (Baker, 2020).
- Loss of worker productivity and engagement; employee turnover is high at mid-career, particularly for college-educated individuals (Hagerty, 2016).

In the following section, I focus on the second bullet point and offer insight into the other individually focused implications most prominent in the literature: job burnout, faculty disengagement, and stalled career progression.

Job Burnout

According to the Mayo Clinic (2020), job burnout is defined as "a special type of work-related stress—a state of physical or emotional exhaustion that also involves a sense of reduced accomplishment and loss of personal identity" (para 1). One of the many problems associated with job burnout is that contributing symptoms occur over time, making it challenging for the individual to realize they are headed toward or firmly in a state of burnout. At the individual level, burnout looks like a cynical or overly critical co-worker, irritable or impatient with others. Job burnout looks like a colleague struggling to concentrate, stay on task, or complete a given task; someone with seemingly no energy or interest in projects, topics, or activities that were once a motivating force. I think many of us have witnessed this firsthand in relation to our colleagues or perhaps, experienced burnout ourselves.

Look no further than the list of contributing factors of job burnout such as loss of control, unclear job expectations, lack of social support, negative leadership behaviors, and work-life imbalance to understand why MCF are in need of support (Cleveland Clinic, 2020; Mayo Clinic, 2020;

Valcour, 2018). These are the very characteristics that have been used by MCF themselves to describe their lived experiences in the academy during this phase of their careers (Baker & Manning, 2021; Mulholland, 2020). The global pandemic has only exacerbated these issues with faculty reporting even higher levels of burnout causing some to consider leaving the academy altogether (Course Hero, 2020). Job burnout is real and has implications at the individual, student, and institutional levels (Minter, 2009; Sabagh et al., 2018).

More recently, scholars have sought to better understand the contributing factors and implications of job burnout for faculty (Sabagh et al., 2018). This line of inquiry has examined the role of organizational and workplace climate (Dinibutun et al., 2020; Pedersen & Minnotte, 2017), work-family conflict (Zábrodská et al., 2018), and job satisfaction and scholarly productivity (Woo et al., 2017) as contributing factors of faculty burnout. Taken as a collective, this line of inquiry revealed that context matters (see Chapter 7), relationships matter (see Chapters 6 and 7), culture matters, and investing in resources and support to help faculty combat burnout matters. When lacking, faculty members' physical and mental well-being suffer.

Faculty Disengagement

Research by Beauboeuf et al. (2017) targeted MCF members in an effort to move past the dominant focus on mid-career malaise to instead focus on the ways in which MCF highlighted the positive aspects of mid-career. Important to their work was a focus on faculty engagement (and disengagement). They found that MCF who participated in their research study focused a great deal on non-material needs, specifically the need to be recognized and to feel and experience a sense of belonging: "To be seen, valued, and included was a critical aspect of their career satisfaction and affected the degree of connection they felt to their campuses" (para 10). The absence of such support resulted in faculty disengagement, which could be linked to institutional practices that leave faculty members feeling undervalued, overcommitted, and expendable (Beauboeuf et al., 2017). No doubt, job burnout is but one contributing factor to faculty disengagement; when left untreated that disengagement comes at a high individual (and institutional) cost.

Recently, a colleague and I wrote an article titled, "Preparing the Next Generation of Institutional Leaders: Strategic Supports for Mid-Career Faculty," to highlight the value and importance of succession management and onboarding. These human resource (HR) tools enable knowledge acquisition, support talent management, and facilitate socialization processes which enable an engaged, committed workforce (Ndunguru, 2012; Rothwell et al., 2015). In brief, these HR tools are the foundation to building a more deliberate, strategic approach to supporting MCF and better equips them to fulfill their leadership roles and responsibilities (Baker & Manning, in press).

Absence of this support results in poorly prepared and ill-equipped faculty members who are unable to meet performance expectations (Baker & Manning, in press). I think there are few things worse in a work context than feeling underprepared and unable to do your job, which is demoralizing and defeating. What is faculty disengagement? It looks like someone who fails to respond to emails or work tasks in a timely manner (if at all). Faculty disengagement describes the faculty colleague who fails to "take their turn" for service needs at the departmental level. It characterizes the colleague who does not contribute in any meaningful way to the classroom, department, or institution. This should alarm us all. As my colleague and I wrote, "While we, as members of the academy, find it unfortunate to lose an amazing colleague, we should be deeply concerned about the disengaged and or poorly prepared faculty member who stays and is tasked with 'leading us' " (Baker & Manning, in press).

Stalled Career Progression

"Mid-career slump," "terminal associate," and "post-tenure letdown" are just a few of the ways in which MCF and this aspect of their career journey have been described in the literature (Dow, 2014; Mathews, 2014; Vongalis-Macrow, 2014; Walsh, 2015). I find this so unfortunate given this career moment of faculty members' paths can be a rebirth, an opportunity to evolve, and to re-envision the next phase of their career. Instead, many MCF experience ambivalence about what move to make next (Kelsky, 2019), and data reveal that a large number of MCF find themselves stalled, particularly women and faculty of color, with little guidance or motivation to move forward (Mathews, 2014; Misra & Lundquist, 2015).

Earlier in my career, I made quite a few assumptions—one of which was that all faculty members on the tenure track had the goal of earning full professorship. This was my aim, and the goal of my closest academic friends and colleagues, so I assumed most academics felt similarly. However, in the process of conducting focus groups and workshops with faculty members, particularly those at mid-career, I learned my assumption was deeply misguided (Baker et al., 2017; www.leadmentordevelop.com). Many faculty described the emotional and physical toll earning P&T had on them; some even talked about the strained familial relationships that resulted. One woman shared that her marriage was unlikely to withstand the six to seven years required to advance to full. This reality meant many felt stalled, resulting in the label of "terminal associate" professor. While some faculty felt dejected by this outcome, seeing no alternative, others were at peace with the decision choosing sanity and mental well-being over a career goal that did not result in additional career benefits beyond a new title/rank (Baker et al., 2017).

Through these interactions I realized the importance of targeted, dedicated developmental support at mid-career. While not all faculty members may aspire to full professorship, I have yet to encounter a faculty member who does not seek to feel fulfilled in their career or contribute in meaningful ways to the stakeholders they hold most dear. Being an expert in one's field as achieved through earning P&T does not mean they are also an expert in career development tools and strategies; support *is* needed.

In sum, MCF must be diligent about their own and others' health and well-being. Mid-career, given the vagueness that accompanies this career stage, has the potential to afflict MCF to varying degrees throughout their experience. By highlighting the issues, contributing factors, and outcomes, we can all better educate ourselves. While it may be impossible to remove the superficial measures of a "stalled career" or institutional level contributing factors to job burnout or faculty disengagement, we *can* recommit to and invest in ourselves as MCF by employing the tools and strategies offered later in this chapter to manage our profession and those we are tasked with supporting.

Returning to Sam's Experience

As a management educator, I rely on case studies and real-world examples to help illustrate main points and achieve the learning lessons I have laid out on any given day. I find that my students' learning is facilitated by seeing the day's principles and concepts in action, requiring us to identify the relevant facts, key stakeholders, and needed information as we seek to make informed decisions and recommendations. In this section of the chapter, I explore the mini-case study at the beginning of the chapter to "analyze" Sam's situation as a way of getting us all to think through steps Sam can pursue, regardless of what supports are, or are not, offered on their campus.

Before we analyze the case together, however, take some time to jot down ideas related to Sam's experience of pursuing full professorship. What stands out to you? What are some positive actions Sam has taken? What information is missing? What questions would you ask Sam? Write those ideas down here before we tackle this academic coaching case together.

_____

_____

_____

_____

_____
_____
_____
_____
_____
_____
_____
_____
_____
_____
_____
_____
_____
_____
_____
_____
_____
_____
_____
_____
_____
_____

Relevant Facts

As with any case analysis, we must first start by identifying the key facts of the case. There a few key facts about Sam's experience that stand out to me. First, Sam is new to mid-career given their more recent (within the past two years) promotion to associate professor. This means we, as academic coaches, have a longer runway to work with as we support Sam's goal achievement. Second, Sam recently completed a sabbatical and shared that all remaining "lingering" pre-tenure projects are now completed, allowing for a "fresh start" on new projects to pursue. Mental health and well-being are both a priority for Sam and something they have and will prioritize as evidenced by taking a year off to recalibrate after earning P&T. Sam's intersecting identities (e.g., recently tenured, LGBTQ, lives in a conservative community beyond the academic campus) are factors in their career journey. Sam leveraged existing networks to educate themselves on advancing to full professorship at their institution; however, that effort resulted in mixed responses, as did a review of existing institutional policies and practices. As a result, Sam is questioning if advancing to full professorship is even worth it.

Key Stakeholders

While Sam is the central actor in this case and the "target" of our focus, there are other stakeholders important to Sam's experience that are both explicitly identified and implicitly absent. First and most evident is Sam's network. Based on what we know, Sam felt comfortable enough to seek advice and guidance from several members from their campus as they work through their advancement to full initial thinking and planning. Those types of conversations require trust and respect. I know I do not seek career advice or guidance from someone I do not trust or that I do not regard as having a strong professional reputation. This circle of peers and colleagues is certainly an advantage for Sam, and something to be further explored and leveraged. Sam does not, however, talk about or to anyone on their campus in a formal leadership role, at least not based on what is provided here. We also do not know what type, if any, disciplinary network Sam has access to as one other potential source of support along their path to full journey.

Needed Information

As I read about Sam's experiences, my academic coach and faculty developer hats immediately go on high alert. Assessing the information available, I have questions about Sam's professional and personal goals first. Yes, on the surface it is clear Sam has an interest in pursuing full professorship, but that pursuit requires engagement and complementary goals across a variety of faculty roles and responsibilities. An academic does not merely pursue full professorship in a vacuum. Rather, full professorship as a professional pursuit requires engagement and action across a variety of areas. This is an area to explore further with Sam.

Second, we do not know much about Sam's professional responsibilities beyond being a faculty member at a comprehensive university. Sam is certainly expected to engage across the triumvirate of teaching, scholarship, and service but the extent to which is unclear. In addition, given their recent P&T, they may be expected to assume a leadership role on campus (e.g., department chair) so consideration must be given to leadership expectations. The bottom line: All of their professional expectations must be factored into any plans for pursuing full professorship. From a scholarly perspective, Sam appears to have a clean slate from which to build. This may, or may not, be advantageous pending Sam's ideas related to scholarly engagement.

Third, we need to help Sam gain clarity about institutional policies and practices related to advancement to full professorship. This includes questions related to (a) promotion criteria, with corresponding definitions and examples; (b) procedural information including who and/

or what (e.g., departmental colleagues, personnel committee, external disciplinary experts) contributes to the process and decision-making; and (c) outcomes of the advancement to full professorship process beyond change in title and rank (e.g., salary increase, access to a select list of leadership roles at the institution). It's imperative to know the rules of the game before you can play it.

Finally, Sam needs support assessing their existing network of mentors in relation to their professional (and personal) goals. This assessment includes an accounting of individuals already in the network, the role(s) they fill in Sam's life (e.g., professional mentor, personal mentor), and who and what (e.g., competencies, social capital) is missing from Sam's network to support their career advancement goals.

Case Summary

I have an advantage in analyzing Sam's case given they are someone with whom I have worked closely as an academic coach on professional pursuits and still engage with regularly. A fellow academic peer introduced me to Sam and provided me with the information shared at the beginning of this chapter. Our mutual colleague emailed us with the hope that I could help Sam "be smart about pursuing full professorship" given my related experiences. What I outline here in terms of related facts, key stakeholders, and needed information are from the initial notes I took following the introductory email. I also include the follow-up questions I emailed Sam, which I planned to work through collaboratively during our first few coaching sessions. The first step, however, was getting a better idea of who Sam was as a professional (and person outside of work) in the present moment, and then helping Sam think thoughtfully and deeply about who they wanted to be in their next professional evolution. In the following section, I offer tools, strategies, and resources to help you gain insight into these aspects as a critical foundation to moving forward.

Tools, Strategies, and Resources

At the start of any coaching engagement or as pre-workshop preparation, I share some guided reflection questions to get individuals thinking about where they currently are professionally (and personally) as a necessary step to mapping out where they want to be. I rely on two foundational activities and associated tools to get this process started: "Fly on the Wall," Modified 360-Degree Assessment, and "Key Contributions." In this section, I walk you through each of the activities along with benefits and usability of the knowledge gleaned.

"Fly on the Wall" and Modified 360-Degree Assessment

In most institutional settings, the path toward P&T hopefully offers some form of regularly scheduled opportunities for developmental feedback that includes insights into present performance accompanied by areas for improvement. For those on the tenure track, these opportunities for feedback may include interim review, P&T review spanning multiple levels (e.g., departmental, committee, institutional, external review), opportunities to meet with members from a personnel committee, and yearly evaluations. Regarding yearly evaluations, I have seen a diversity of approaches employed across institution types. Examples range from deeply collaborative between the early career colleague and department chair, mapping out goals and growth opportunities together, to a mere categorical listing of what the faculty member has "accomplished" in the past year (e.g., teaching, research, and service) with no accompanying performance assessment.

After earning P&T, however, these more formalized opportunities to secure feedback from interdisciplinary peers or a range of individuals is greatly reduced. Yet, understanding how we are perceived and viewed in our various contexts is important to advancing toward career goals. Feedback that includes others' assessments unencumbered by issues of impression management, particularly at mid-career, is even better. Given this, I urge you to respond to the following question(s):

Fly on the Wall

1   If you were a fly on the wall, listening to others describe you as a teacher, scholar, campus/community contributor, or any other roles pertinent to you (e.g., parent, partner, or friend), what would they say? You need to be honest with yourself as you respond. Note any critiques (positive or negative) that you are aware of, including those that you suspect might be on the forefront of the minds of those with whom you most interact.

_____

_____

_____

_____

_____

_____

_____

_____

_____

_____

_____

_____

_____

_____

_____

_____

_____

_____

_____

_____

_____

Now, I offer the same question, with a slight adjustment. Respond to:

2   If you were a fly on the wall, listening to others describe you as a teacher, scholar, campus/community contributor, or any other roles pertinent to you, what do you *want* them to say? Here, think about the reputation you *want* to have and the way(s) you want to be regarded across the various areas in which you engage professionally and personally.

_____

_____

_____

_____

_____

_____

_____

_____

_____

_____

_____

_____

_____

_____

_____

_____

As you engage in a quick scan of your responses to both of these questions, do you note differences in how you are perceived versus how you want to be regarded? If yes, are there certain roles in which you see those differences most prominently? Think thoughtfully about what this insight tells you and how you can act on it. This knowledge will be instrumental to you as we work through goal setting and planning activities outlined in Chapter 2.

Returning to Sam, they found this exercise illuminating. Responses surfaced some disconnects between perceptions and wants. For example, Sam realized that while their students saw them as open, willing to provide support and assistance when needed, Sam believed his colleagues might not share that same opinion and they could understand why, in some instances. Collaboratively, we highlighted these disconnects and sought to make sense of them during our coaching sessions as we mapped out plans to minimize these identified disconnects. It became obvious to Sam that they would need to manage perceptions and be more proactive about building the reputation they wanted to have on campus.

Modified 360-Degree Assessment

To complement this exercise, I strongly encourage you to engage in a Modified 360-degree Assessment, which is a performance appraisal tool used regularly at the leadership and executive levels to secure performance feedback from a diversity of stakeholders including those who are direct reports, organizational peers, and supervisors (Taylor, 2011). The goal is to secure feedback from those with whom you work most closely. The assessment can provide direct insight about your abilities as a supervisor, leader and manager, peer, and as a subordinate yourself.

Mid-career is a good time to rethink who these stakeholders are for you; who can provide you with critical insights as you work toward achieving career goals. Of course, some obvious individuals include students, departmental colleagues, and your department chair. However, my guess is you secure some form of feedback from these stakeholder groups already to some capacity (e.g., teaching evaluations, yearly evaluations). I want to push you to reach out to colleagues across campus that are not the obvious choices. Ask the early career colleague across campus what it is like working with you on a campus committee. Ask a staff member from the registrar's office or student affairs department to share insights on your most valuable contributions or ways you could better utilize your talents to support campus initiatives or programs. Engage alumni from the past five to 10 years who worked with you to assess their experience working with you; what are your strengths and what are some growth opportunities? You could also consider including a disciplinary peer with whom you most interact with through professional associations. The goal is to secure feedback from a diversity of individuals for whom you are not likely to gather regular feedback.

The combination of feedback from these two complementary activities forces you to engage in an internally focused self-assessment and to compare your perceived reality of how you are viewed versus aspirational goals for how you want to be regarded by institutional peers and campus leaders. Others' perceptions and beliefs about you, however accurate and fair (or not) factor into advancement opportunities on your respective campus. You need to know where you stand in relation. Further, supplementing that insight with actual feedback from a small group of individuals you engage with via a modified 360-degree assessment serves as an excellent foundation and provides explicit, accurate insights from which to build. The following are questions you might consider including in your modified 360-degree assessment:

- What are my strengths?
- What is one area of professional strength that I do not leverage or use as much as I should?
- What are the areas in which I can further develop?
- What opportunities should I be seeking on campus (community, field) to further develop in areas of need?
- What advice do you have for me as I focus on areas most important to short and long development?

Remember, ask no more than three to five targeted questions and be sure to diversify the stakeholder groups represented. Be sure those individuals are not people for which you receive feedback with some regularity.

Returning to Sam's experience, I think it is fair to say that they were intimidated at first by this activity. Moreover, quite honestly, Sam was apprehensive about doing it. However, they were willing to try. We relied on the disconnects identified from the "Fly on the Wall" exercise to help select (and invite) individuals who would be thoughtful, developmental, and honest in their assessments. The feedback collected from the

Modified 360-Degree Assessment informed a wealth of growth and professional developmental opportunities that really ignited Sam's eagerness to pursue next steps in their professional journey. One such example was Sam developing and delivering an active learning strategies workshop through the Center for Teaching and Learning which both displayed their content knowledge and expertise while increasing campus visibility.

Key Contribution(s)

Now that you have some insight into how you are/want to be perceived, real and aspirational, it is a good time to take a step back and take a broader view of your career and life. The next question I ask of my coaching clients and workshop attendees (as well as ask of myself with some regularity) takes more of a 10,000 foot view of where they/I want to be and how they/I want to be regarded in terms of professional (and personal) contributions.

1 Again, get your pen/pencil ready, and write down thoughts to the following question: At this phase of your career, what do you want your contribution to be?

_____

_____

_____

_____

_____

_____

_____

_____

_____

_____

_____

_____

_____

_____

_____

_____

_____

_____

_____

_____

_____

_____

_____

_____

_____

_____

_____

_____

_____

_____

_____

_____

_____

_____

_____

_____

_____

This is a critically important question to me; one that at my core fundamentally drives my professional and personal choices. As I was moving toward and firmly situated in mid-career, I engaged in some serious moments of self-reflection and assessment of myself as a professional and as a mother, wife, daughter, and friend. I was knocking it out of the park professionally, in fact so much so that my P&T review decision letter noted concern that the pace at which I was producing in teaching, scholarship, and service were unsustainable. The committee members were right, as I was falling short in my personal roles; self-care was nonexistent and I was struggling to find work-life balance, which I still do not believe in nor do I think is attainable (to me, it's about prioritizing moments). I took a step back and asked myself, what do I want my contribution to be?

As I think about where I find the most joy and what I am most passionate about, the drivers of my professional and personal choices (Baker, 2020), I realized that my contribution can best be stated as "I want to help others advance in their careers." I put that statement in writing and then asked myself the following questions: How can I help others' advance in their careers through my teaching? How can I help others' advance in their careers through my scholarship? How can I help others' advance in their careers through my service? How can I help others' advance in their careers through my consulting and academic coaching? How can I help my kids/family members advance in their careers in my role as mother/wife/daughter?

I use these questions to help guide course revisions or as I evaluate service opportunities on campus (as I decide what to say yes to). If a given activity or action I am taking is not in service to my intended contribution and the subsequent reflection questions, I take extra time to evaluate why I am even considering it. The global pandemic has only heightened the importance of this activity and the need to take a personal and professional inventory of where I currently spend my time. If those activities are not in service to my intended contribution, I have all but eliminated them from my to-do list—a commitment that will last far beyond the aftermath of COVID-19.

2 Using the above questions as a guide, re-write your contribution similarly in the context/roles most relevant to you. You can use "how" queries to ignite the process.

_____

_____

_____

_____

_____

_____

_____

_____

_____

_____

_____

_____

_____

_____

_____

_____

_____

_____

_____

_____

_____

Chapter Summary and Next Steps

The main aim of this chapter is to highlight a critical problem MCF faculty face as they enter this phase of their careers: **A lack of clearly defined career hurdles and developmental milestones.** Several factors contribute to this problem; most notable is because the mid-career career stage is the longest career stage. Given the length of time, many MCF members experience, to varying degrees, job burnout and feelings of disengagement as they struggle to maneuver this phase of the professoriate. For some, this phase results in a "stalled career," albeit by choice for some as they weigh the benefits and costs of pursuing full professorship or other aspirations such as administrative posts. I hope the individual outcomes featured in the chapter help alert you to the signs and symptoms associated with job burnout, disengagement, and stalled career progression so you can both help yourself and your colleagues who too are grappling with these issues. Creating a mid-career community elevates this career stage and supports the teachers, scholars, leaders, and innovators who hold up their institutions daily.

While not without challenges, mid-career is ripe with opportunity, and signals a time to reflect intentionally about reimagining one's career evolution. It is about re-writing the mid-career narrative; one in which career planning is aspirational, rooted in joy, full of passion, and focused on the professional and personal areas most valued. It is possible to advance toward career goals, in spite of a lack of clear career stage milestone. It happens when MCF take ownership and ask for (and receive) the needed support.

As stated, I believe it critically important to have a clear understanding of where you currently are in order to advance to where you aspire to be. The guided reflection questions and Modified 360-degree Assessment featured will offer critical insight, and serves as a foundation from which to build moving forward. Write down ideas right on the pages offered throughout this chapter, refer to them often, and use them as catalysts to propel you toward your dreams. Writing down your dreams and goals *is* the first step. In fact, keep your notes from this chapter nearby as we dive into more targeted strategic planning and goal setting in Chapter 2.

References

Baker, V. L., Lunsford, L. G., & Pifer, M. J. (2017). *Developing faculty in liberal arts colleges: Aligning individual needs and organizational goals.* Rutgers University Press.

Baker, V. L., Lunsford, L. G., & Pifer, M. J. (2019). Patching up the "leaking leadership pipeline": Fostering mid-career faculty succession management. *Research in Higher Education, 60*(6), 823–843.

Baker, V. L. (2020). *Charting your path to full: A guide for women associate professors.* Rutgers University Press.

Baker, V. L., & Manning, C. E. (2021). A mid-career faculty agenda: A review of four decades of research and practice. *Higher Education: Handbook of Theory and Research: Volume 36*, 1–66.

Baker. V. L., & Manning, C. E. N. (in press). Preparing the next generation of institutional leaders: Strategic supports for mid-career faculty. *To Improve the Academy.*Baldwin, R. G., & Chang, D. A. (2006). Reinforcing our "keystone" faculty: Strategies to support faculty in the middle years of academic life. *Liberal Education, 92*(4), 28–35.

Beauboeuf, T., Thomas, J. E., & Erickson, K. A. (2017). Our fixation on midcareer malaise. *The Chronicle of Higher Education.* www.chronicle.com/article/our-fixation-on-midcareer-malaise/?cid2=gen_login_refresh&cid=gen_sign_in

Cleveland Clinic (April 10, 2020). 7 red flags of job burnout – and what you can do.https://health.clevelandclinic.org/7-red-flags-of-job-burnout-and-what-you-can-do/

Course Hero (2020). Faculty fear permanent changes, experienced increases burnout caused by COVID-19. *Cision PR Newswire.* www.prnewswire.com/news-releases/faculty-fear-permanent-changes-experience-increased-burnout-caused-by-covid-19-301177068.html.

Dinibutun, S. R., Kuzey, C., & Dinc, M. S. (2020). The effect of organizational climate on faculty burnout at state and private universities: A comparative analysis. *SAGE Open, 10*(4), 2158244020979175.

Dow, N. (March 26, 2014). Terminal associate professors, past and present. *The Chronicle of Higher Education.* www.chronicle.com/article/terminal-associate-professors-past-and-present/?cid2=gen_login_refresh&cid=gen_sign_in.

Flaherty, C. (January 26, 2017). Midcareer professors need love, too. *Inside HigherEd.* www.insidehighered.com/news/2017/01/26/research-midcareer-professors-makes-case-support-after-tenure.

Gibbons, S. (March 20, 2018). Many employees have a mid-career crisis. Here's how employers can help. *Harvard Business Review.* https://hbr.org/2018/03/many-employees-have-a-mid-career-crisis-heres-how-employers-can-help

Grant-Vallone, E. J., & Ensher, E. A. (2017). Re-crafting careers for mid-career faculty: A qualitative study. *Journal of Higher Education Theory and Practice, 17*(5), 10–24.

Hagerty, B. B. (April, 2016). Quit your job: A midlife career shift can be good for cognition, well-being, and even longevity. *The Atlantic.* www.theatlantic.com/magazine/archive/2016/04/quit-your-job/471501/

Kelsky, K. (April 18, 2019). The professor is in: Ambivalence about midcareer moves. *The Chronicle of Higher Education.* https://community.chronicle.com/news/2187-the-professor-is-in-ambivalence-about-midcareer-moves

Mathews, K. R. (2014). Perspectives on midcareer faculty and advice for supporting them. *The Collaborative on Academic Careers in Higher Education.* https://scholar.harvard.edu/files/kmathews/files/coache_mathews_midcareerfaculty_20140721.pdf

Mayo Clinic (November 20, 2020). Job burnout: How to spot it and take action. www.mayoclinic.org/healthy-lifestyle/adult-health/in-depth/burnout/art-20046642#:~:text=Job%20burnout%20is%20a%20special,isn't%20a%20medical%20diagnosis

Minsky, L., & Peters, J. T. (September 5, 2019). Are you at risk of a mid-career rut. *Harvard Business Review.* https://hbr.org/2019/09/are-you-at-risk-of-a-mid-career-rut

Minter, R. L. (2009). Faculty burnout. *Contemporary Issues in Education Research, 2*(2), 1–8.

Misra, J. & Lundquist, J. (June 26, 2015). Diversity and the ivory ceiling. *Inside HigherEd.* www.insidehighered.com/advice/2015/06/26/essay-diversity-issues-and-midcareer-faculty-members

Mulholland, J. (Winter, 2020). Slow down: On dealing with mid-career burnout. *MLA Profession.* https://profession.mla.org/slow-down-on-dealing-with-midcareer-burnout/

Ndunguru, C. A. (2012). Executive onboarding: How to hit the ground running. *Public Manager, 41*(3), 6–9.

Pedersen, D. E., & Minnotte, K. L. (2017). Workplace climate and STEM faculty women's job burnout. *Journal of Feminist Family Therapy, 29*(1–2), 45–65.

Perry, D. M. (June 23, 2014). But does it count? *The Chronicle of Higher Education.* www.chronicle.com/article/but-does-it-count/?cid2=gen_login_refresh&cid=gen_sign_in

Rothwell, W. J., Jackson, R. D., Ressler, C. L., Jones, M. C., & Brower, M. (2015). *Career planning and succession management: Developing your organization's talent—for today and tomorrow.* ABC-CLIO.

Sabagh, Z., Hall, N. C., & Saroyan, A. (2018). Antecedents, correlates and consequences of faculty burnout. *Educational Research, 60*(2), 131–156.

Strage, A., & Merdinger, J. (2015). Professional growth and renewal for mid-career faculty. *The Journal of Faculty Development, 29*(1), 41–50.

Strunk, K. K. (March 13, 2020). Demystifying and democratizing tenure and promotion. *Inside HigherEd.* www.insidehighered.com/advice/2020/03/13/tenure-and-promotion-process-must-be-revised-especially-historically-marginalized

Taylor, S. (July 12, 2011). Assess pros and cons of 360-degree performance appraisal. *Society for Human Resource Management.* www.shrm.org/resourcesandtools/hr-topics/employee-relations/pages/360degreeperformance.aspx

Valcour, M (January 25, 2018). When burnout is a sign you should leave your job. *Harvard Business Review.* https://hbr.org/2018/01/when-burnout-is-a-sign-you-should-leave-your-job

Vongalis-Macrow, A. (Ed.) (2014). Avoiding mid-career stalling. In *Career moves: Mentoring for women advancing their career and leadership in academia* (pp. 71–82). Sense Publishers.

Walsh, B. (April 6, 2015). Battling the midcareer slump: How college can cultivate a vital and engaged faculty throughout their careers. *Harvard Graduate School of Education.* www.gse.harvard.edu/news/uk/15/04/battling-midcareer-slump

Woo, H., Park, S., & Kim, H. (2017). Job satisfaction as a moderator on the relationship between burnout and scholarly productivity among counseling faculty in the US. *Asia Pacific Education Review, 18*(4), 573–583.

Zábrodská, K., Mudrák, J., Šolcová, I., Květon, P., Blatný, M., & Machovcová, K. (2018). Burnout among university faculty: The central role of work–family conflict. *Educational Psychology, 38*(6), 800–819.

Chapter 2

Planning, Goal-Setting, and Problem Solving

Sarah, a humanities faculty member in a liberal arts college, has been at the associate professor rank for just over seven years now. She loves teaching, loves her students, and loves the "vibrant community" she and her family live in. In her words, she "soaks up all that she can by engaging with her students," and she is "in awe" of how brilliant they really are. Much like other MCF at her institution and in her field, she was both exhilarated and exhausted by the tenure and promotion process. Couple that with the amount of work and energy she invests in her teaching and mentoring of students, and it takes its toll. So far, she has managed to avoid assuming formal leadership positions on campus, most notably department chair. She knows it will be "her turn" in the near future, but it is not anything Sarah is necessarily looking forward to, though "she will do her duty" when the time comes. Until recently, Sarah was not interested in seeking full professorship, at least not while her children were preschool age. However, Sarah's kids are older now, and Sarah is revisiting the notion of pursuing full professorship. Once she started reviewing the faculty development programming at her institution, however, she was reminded of one of the reasons she opted out in the first place. Based on a list of previous programs on the faculty resources page (including the Center for Teaching and Learning), Sarah could only find one formal program targeted at mid-career. After asking around if this list was outdated, she was informed that the information was both accurate and up-to-date. Feeling deflated, Sarah realized it was time to figure out what she really wants to do (and why). Yet, Sarah was not sure where to begin.

DOI: 10.4324/9781003201311-4

Sarah's experience and feelings highlight something so many of us face at one point or another throughout our careers—confronting that all too familiar crossroads where we ask ourselves, what do I want to do, why do I want to do it, and how am I going to do it? This crossroads is notorious for surfacing during mid-career and requires support and guidance to traverse it effectively. Unfortunately, most institutions offer **limited dedicated resources and developmental programming aimed at mid-career,** the featured problem in this chapter. Couple this reality with a lack of career milestones (the featured problem in Chapter 1) and you have the perfect storm in which talented individuals struggle to find their professional way, and the academy misses out on those possible contributions.

The questions Sarah faces are not easy to answer, nor do they have easy solutions. Throughout this chapter, I focus on the contributing factors and implications for mid-career faculty (MCF) when there is a lack of dedicated resources and programming to assist them as they navigate the proverbial professional crossroads that accompanies mid-career. As we learned in Chapter 1, engaged employees are productive, fulfilled employees. To navigate the mid-career stage, MCF need to have clear goals, plans, and resources to facilitate effective career planning and problem solving. The tools, resources, and strategies featured in this chapter are fundamental to facing *and* overcoming the mid-career crossroads.

Why Are There so Few Dedicated Resources or Programming Geared at Mid-Career?

My colleagues and I engaged in a longitudinal study of a consortium of 13 liberal arts colleges about the faculty experience (Baker et al., 2017). Our initial study included faculty from all disciplines and ranks, allowing us to learn more about the faculty experience as a whole in liberal arts colleges and to start identifying unique needs and challenges associated with career ranks/stages and discipline (Baker et al., 2018). Upon analyzing the data, the most prominent issues arose among MCF; the challenges they faced were unique, expansive, and connected to a myriad roles and responsibilities. Based on the data, we realized the importance of learning more about mid-career to target needed supports and interventions. Bottom line—the MCF employed at these institutions needed support, and we assumed campus leaders and faculty administrators could use the guidance.

As the necessary next step, we proposed a targeted MCF mixed-methods study, which included faculty as well as administrators and campus leaders across these liberal arts college campuses. We pitched the idea at a consortium-level meeting attended by 13 deans and secured their approval and overwhelmingly positive support to move forward with the research. As part of this research, we learned that MCF were eager for faculty development programming and resources aimed at helping them manage the diversity of expectations placed upon them. We also learned that campus leaders and administrators believed deeply in the importance of their MCF and saw the value in offering more targeted programming to this population of faculty. One of the most compelling yet discouraging findings from this study was that despite this shared agreement about the significance of investing in targeted mid-career programming, there was limited to no programming that met these needs or priorities (Baker et al., 2016). It caused my colleagues and me to wonder—why are there so few dedicated resources or programming geared at mid-career?

Simply stated, the mid-career stage does not happen in a vacuum. A range of contextual factors contribute to the experiences of MCF, ranging from the local community (e.g., department, institution, surrounding neighborhood) to the field of higher education more broadly. Additionally, disciplinary nuances; evolving professional expectations, methodologies, and pedagogies; and the rapid pace at which technology changes create moving targets for faculty and the individuals with faculty development responsibilities. Working to account for all of these contributing factors can become overwhelming quickly, and may result in opting out entirely rather than starting with a few targeted programs to support MCF. In the following section, I highlight some of the most notable challenges in higher education that influence the experiences of MCF.

Evolving Nature of Higher Education

The field of higher education has experienced quite a significant evolution, and those changes have a direct impact on the faculty experience. Dating back to the 1960s, higher education was characterized by its expansion. Consistently climbing enrollment figures, the creation of new universities, and the presence of academic entrepreneurism defined higher education for several decades (Vedder, 2017). There were more faculty employed in higher education institutions compared to administrative staff (Snyder, 1993), and faculty had more power to make decisions about university life and the direction of the institution (Vedder, 2017).

Today, however, the growth that once characterized higher education has dissipated. In fact, student enrollment is declining overall (St. Amour, 2020), as is the graduation rate among high school students, which equates into fewer students pursuing higher education (Wiley, 2021). For those students who do pursue higher education, the costs are significant. Couple enrollment challenges with greater reliance on federal and state funding, which too is dwindling (Pew Charitable Trust, 2019), and campus leaders are faced with challenges that require tough decisions about where to invest resources. The COVID-19 global pandemic only served to exacerbate these challenges (Polikoff et al., 2020). Abrupt shifts to online learning were required as questions arose about how to provide student services remotely to support the educational experience. Already challenged financial situations worsened as students left their respective campuses with little clarity about when and how they would return.

At the core of these challenges are the faculty members who I characterize as the front line workers in higher education, tasked with delivering the education to enrolled students. It was those same faculty members who were required to adapt their educational delivery models with little runway or support to do so. They served as teachers, mentors, counselors, technology specialists, and more to their students. Those faculty members with more online teaching experience were also called upon to mentor colleagues with less online experience. Yet, faculty and professional development funds were some of the first resources cut from budgets across higher education in response. I argued in two recent opinion pieces that the opposite should be happening (Baker, 2020a; Baker, 2020b). It appears we sometimes lose sight of how important faculty really are in higher education, especially in times of crisis. The lack of investments made to support our veteran faculty colleagues became even more pronounced during the global pandemic.

Lack of Diversity in the Professoriate

In addition to funding and enrollment challenges, a lack of diversity in higher education remains a concern. Over the past four decades, educators and campus leaders began to recognize the value of racial and ethnic diversity and the importance of that diversity to student learning, development, and growth (Bouchrika, 2020). In 1980, students of color made up approximately 17 percent of enrolled undergraduate students (National Center for Education Statistics, 2018). According to a report published by American Council on Education, that figure has risen to 42 percent (Espinosa et al., 2019).

Recent data, however, paints a different picture of the professoriate. Research by Espinosa and colleagues (2019), for example, revealed diversity among faculty ranks does not mirror the diversity represented at the undergraduate student level in U.S. postsecondary education. Data reveal the academy is still predominantly White and male. As of fall 2018, approximately 40 percent of full-time faculty were White males, 35 percent were White females; 7 percent were Asian/Pacific Islander males, 5 percent were Asian/Pacific Islander females; 3 percent were Black males, Black females, Hispanic males, and Hispanic females. Less than one percent of faculty were American Indian/Alaska Native. See Table 2.1 for a demographic breakdown by faculty rank.

Table 2.1 Demographic Breakdown of Faculty by Rank (National Center for Education Statistics, 2018)

	Full Professor	Associate Professor	Assistant Professor
White	53/27	40/35	34/39
Asian/Pacific Islander	8/3	7/5	7/7
Black	2/2	3/3	3/5
Hispanic	2/1	3/2	3/3

Note: Figures are percentages; males/females.

Increased Reliance of Contingent Faculty

Another important trend that affects the faculty experience and access to needed faculty development supports is increased reliance on the use of non-tenure track (NTT), contingent faculty across the academy. According to research conducted by the American Association of University Professors (AAUP), in 2016 postsecondary institutions hired 30,865 full-time, non-tenure-track instructional faculty members, compared to 21,511 full-time, tenure-track professors (Flaherty, 2018). In fact, NTT positions of all types (e.g., full-time, part-time, adjunct NTT) now account for over 70 percent of all instructional staff appointments in American higher education (AAUP, 2018). While the highest percentage of contingent faculty appears at two-year institutions (tenure-track positions account for less than 20 percent of faculty positions), the use of contingent faculty is on the rise across all institution types (AAUP, 2014; Kezar et al., 2016). This shift in faculty employment models not only has implications for the faculty members themselves in terms of career satisfaction and job security, but also has negative consequences for student learning and development (Hurlburt & McGarrah, 2016). Kezar and colleagues write, "Arguably, these outcomes stem from institutions' failure to properly support this growing segment of the faculty" (2016, p. 4).

The challenges and opportunities associated with the MCF stage (Baker & Manning, 2021) as well as those associated with NTT and adjunct faculty appointments have garnered research and practice attention over the past decade (Kezar, 2012; Waltman et al., 2012; Yakoboski, 2015). However, we have very limited knowledge and understanding about the intersection of career stage and faculty appointment type. In our meta-synthesis involving a four decades review of research and practice on MCF (Baker & Manning, 2021), we were only able to find one study that examined the impact of career stage on adjunct faculty (Feldman & Turnley, 2001). Their findings revealed that "career stage did have a significant impact on the dependent variables" (Feldman & Turnley, 2001, p. 9), resulting in positive and negative implications at mid-career.

While contingent positions can provide opportunities for creativity and autonomy at mid-career, adjunct positions resulted in widespread carry-over of professional responsibilities into personal time. This carryover makes it challenging to plan for the future, respond to career demands of a partner or spouse, and operate without disruptions due to the lack of a reliable and consistent schedule.

Higher education is evolving rapidly and faculty members are required to be change agents. However, resources and developmental programming to help faculty rise to the occasion is lacking, especially at mid-career. The global pandemic required swift action by all members of the academy. That swift action revealed higher education, as a field, could innovate quickly when needed and that same mindset can be applied to advancing the field of faculty development. Now is the time to innovate faculty development to account for the realities of the academy and disciplinary advances. Such investment will enable MCF to progress in their careers while contributing much needed knowledge and expertise.

Returning to Sarah's Experience

Let's discuss Sarah' experience more, featured at the beginning of this chapter, to better understand the implications of a lack of dedicated resources and programming targeted toward mid-career. Understanding how to manage your career, in spite of a lack of formal institutional supports is critical to advancing your own goals and aspirations. There are several tools and resources that can both honor the tasks and roles Sarah holds most dear, while also advancing in her career based on institutional expectations.

Before we analyze Sarah's experience together, pull out a pen or pencil and record your own observations. What are some of the critical "data points" that help us understand Sarah's positionality, context, passions, and goals? Based on what we know, what questions arise for you? What is missing that we need clarity on in order to direct Sarah appropriately? Write down those observations and thoughts now.

_____

_____

_____

_____

_____

_____

_____

_____

_____

_____

_____

_____

_____

_____

_____

_____

_____

_____

_____

_____

_____

_____

Similar to how we analyzed Sam's situation in Chapter 1, to better understand Sarah's experience, we need to think about three areas: Relevant facts, key stakeholders, and needed information.

Relevant Facts

Sarah is a faculty member in the humanities department at a liberal arts college, which means teaching is a dominant responsibility as determined by institutional mission. We know Sarah "loves" teaching, and based on how she describes her relationships with students, we can surmise Sarah is quite engaged with her students. Sarah is a more seasoned MCF member, or what I refer to as a late MCF member (Baker et al., 2017; Mathews, 2014) who made conscious choices about her timeline to full professor. In fact, pursuing full professor was not an aspiration of hers due to having young children at home; she only recently began to think about if full professorship is a goal she wants to pursue. Sarah also did some preliminary research at her institution to determine what, if any, resources were available to support her advancement to full, should she choose to go down that path. Met with limited support by way of programming offered at her institution, Sarah is struggling with where or how to begin thinking about what advancement to full will look like for her and has some reservations about this career goal, in general.

Key Stakeholders

While Sarah is certainly the focus of our attention, there are other key stakeholders relevant to Sarah's experience that will need to be factored into any career advancement plans mapped out. Clearly, her students are very important to her. She makes a point to share insights about the high regard with which she holds her students. She also cares deeply and appreciates the "vibrant community" she lives in, which certainly factors into her overall experiences as a faculty member at her institution. Sarah also has two, school-aged children at home. In fact, her children factored into her decision to not pursue full professorship after earning P&T. Instead, she opted to wait until they were both in school to entertain any career advancement plans. Based on the information provided, Sarah reached out to some colleagues to make sure her "research" into MCF programming on her campus was accurate, but it is unclear who those individuals were (e.g., departmental peers, campus-peers, campus leaders). Finally, she also sought support from a diversity of places, such as the faculty resources page and her college's Center for Teaching and Learning. Her research confirmed that there really is limited, dedicated mid-career supports or programming available on her campus.

Needed Information

As a faculty member myself at a liberal arts college, I know that teaching takes up a substantial amount of the workweek for all faculty members. From the information provided here, however, Sarah's teaching load remains unclear. Her number of courses in a given year can range from five (e.g., 2-3 teaching load) to eight (4-4 teaching load). Sarah's schedule certainly plays a critical role in how she manages career advancement plans. In fact, her teaching responsibilities (including classroom, student hours, advising) need to be at the center of any career advancement plan. Ideally, her teaching roles and responsibilities can be the foundation from which we build a career advancement plan.

Second, similar to Sam in Chapter 1, we do not know much about Sarah's other responsibilities beyond teaching. Even though the mission of a liberal arts college puts teaching as the highest priority, scholarship and service are quite important to varying degrees. We also do not know if Sarah has any current scholarly projects in hand or in the planning stages. Scholarly productivity, even in a liberal arts college, can factor into full professorship decisions quite heavily. In addition, as many faculty in liberal arts colleges know (and is my own experience), we are often one of a few, or the only, faculty member on our respective campuses who teach what we teach. This means, Sarah has to cover both the depth and breadth of a given disciplinary area in her field. This is a lot of responsibility to manage, in addition to all the other responsibilities on and off campus. We need to learn more about how Sarah engages as a faculty member across these areas and what informs her related decision-making.

Third, while Sarah does not mention anything about related institutional policies on her campus (e.g., process for advancing to full), we need to determine if Sarah has this knowledge in hand or if she needs it. As mentioned in Chapter 1, you cannot play the game if you do not know the rules. She did conduct some research into available supports for MCF as a starting point, but ensuring she knows the process including timeline, key stakeholders, and required materials is important to ensuring she has the needed information to make an informed decision about whether she wants to pursue full professorship.

Lastly, we have no idea if Sarah has a network of mentors. If she does, we need to know who those individuals are, and the role they play in helping Sarah advance professionally (and personally). If she does not have a network of mentors, this information is yet another opportunity in which support and guidance can be provided to Sarah including how to cultivate a network of mentors that are both critical to advancement to full and any other professional (or personal) goals for which she aspires. This network is particularly important at a liberal arts college given departmental sizes are typically small, which can be isolating when you are the only person on your campus who does what you do.

Case Summary

I worked with Sarah closely to pursue full professorship (spoiler alert—she earned it). The relevant facts, key stakeholders, and needed information factored into the plans we mapped out collaboratively for Sarah. I should also mention that plan was an "accelerated plan" toward full professorship (three years from the time I started working with her) given she was already at the associate professor rank for seven years when we connected. Our plans were very targeted and built around her love of teaching, her community engagement, and most important, her role as mother (and primary caregiver). Her time was precious; therefore, all the plans we mapped out collaboratively had to be specific and very focused. We relied on the tools, strategies, and resources described in the following section as foundational to her career advancement pursuits.

Tools, Strategies, and Resources

In Chapter 1, the focus was on building the foundation by helping you gain more clarity about the way you are perceived on your respective campus or discipline compared to how you want to be regarded as a teacher, scholar, and community contributor. This knowledge is paramount to advancing toward professional goals. Let's continue this work through three activities: Post Hoc Year in Review, Strategic Professional

Planning, and Problem Solving. These tactics are aimed at managing those inevitable bumps in the road that arise throughout career progression.

Post Hoc Year in Review

One of the biggest challenges I have experienced in my career to date is a lack of time to debrief and reflect on my progress and missteps. There are no formal offerings at my institution or disciplinary association to support this process nor was I as intentional and consistent as I could be early in my career. Engaging in a self-assessment is valuable, and I employ such strategies in the classroom to debrief lessons and assignments, as well as in my roles as mentor and advisor to my undergraduate students. I also build in dedicated time and activities in my capacity as an academic coach with clients. However, taking the time to assess my own progress and engage in the control function or feedback loops as we management educators refer to it is one of the first "to do" items from the list that takes a backseat. It was not until I hit mid-career when I truly realized the power of assessing the areas in which I was investing in my professional and personal pursuits. Such efforts help you determine what is, and is not, going well and provides opportunities to make needed adjustments along the way. No one wants to find out a particular initiative was not worth the investment until after it is over. Not only can that be a great deal of wasted time and resources, it can feel disappointing and demoralizing.

To help facilitate a self-assessment, I propose an activity I refer to as a Post Hoc Year in Review. The phrase "Year in Review" likely conjures some familiarity to you. We often see publications from *TIME* and *Forbes* or news broadcasts from shows such as 60 Minutes, in which major events and memorable moments from the past year are highlighted. The featured events and memories span feel-good stories and catastrophes, given all played a role in how the previous year was defined. The same can be said for our careers and personal lives; there have been many times in my life where my personal life was amazing, and my professional life was not where I wanted it to be and vice versa. However, each event defines a year in your life. As shared in Chapter 1, in order to get where you want to be, you need to know where you have been and where you currently stand.

1 Take out your pen or pencil, and respond to the following: Looking back on the past year, what events stand out to you? First focus on the positive—consider this your highlight reel of successes. Write them down. Be sure to include notes about these events (e.g., the people involved, the focus of the work, the benefit to the end user, made you feel like you really made a difference, and so on).

_____
_____
_____
_____
_____
_____
_____
_____
_____
_____
_____
_____
_____
_____
_____
_____
_____
_____
_____
_____
_____
_____
_____
_____
_____
_____

Take a moment to look at this list. What stands out to you? Are there any patterns in terms of the types of events, the focus of the activity, the individuals involved? Analyze your own actions and performance in relation to these events and activities. Do you see or recollect any similarities? Try to identify a common core or theme that ties these items together. Jot down those observations.

2 Next, reflect on the negative. Look back on the past year and ask yourself: What events activities, responsibilities, and roles stand out to for negative reasons? Be sure to both list the event, activity, or issue and offer some corresponding detail such as who was involved, the focus of the activity/experience/event, or the beneficiary. Write these observations down in the space provided.

_____
_____
_____

_____

_____

_____

_____

_____

_____

_____

_____

_____

_____

Do you see any patterns? What stands out to you from this list? Is this list longer than the list in which successes were highlighted? Hopefully not, but if it is, you need to take a long look at that list and make some adjustments such as eliminating certain activities from your schedule or re-thinking projects and the time commitment allotted. If you are anything like me, some years that negative list is longer than the positive list. That is OK because you are taking the first step at adding more positive events and activities to your calendar moving forward.

The ultimate goal of this activity is to ensure you are taking time to reflect on and assess the areas in which you engage most frequently, and to determine if your highlight reel is one for which to be proud. These events should also make an appearance in dossier materials (so keep this list readily available). The majority of your activities and areas in which you spend your time should be in service to your professional (and personal) pursuits. If this is not a highlight reel you would want the public to see, it is time to reassess where, how, and with whom you are investing your time.

Sarah completed this activity early during our client-academic coach relationship. When she saw on paper all the ways in which she was giving back to her students, department, and institution, Sarah found the activity both helpful and illuminating. She realized how much she gave in areas that took away from more significant goals, such as family time and scholarship. Sarah referred to these black-and-white activities as, "the wakeup call I needed to get clarity on where I am spending my time."

While she does not regret investing her energies in those areas, Sarah also realized that if she were to earn full professorship, she would need to make adjustments to ensure the needed time to pursue her scholarly interests without sacrificing time with family. With Sarah, we were able to identify commonalities across the activities and roles she occupies, in which she felt positive about her contributions. Then, we worked to ensure the other areas we built into her professional plans both involved those areas and expanded on the ways in which she was investing her time.

Professional Strategic Planning

Now that you have completed your Post Hoc Year in Review, it is time to take that knowledge and build a professional strategic plan around it. Strategic planning is an organizational management activity that helps leaders set priorities, allocate resources and attention, and direct employees and shareholders toward common goals (Collins, 2001. However, strategic planning can also be a tool adapted for individual use as you pursue career goals and advancement opportunities. In this section, I walk you through what I refer to as Professional Strategic Planning, specifically how to focus on opportunities, achieve needed results, and identify interim deadlines and deliverables.

Opportunities

As part of your Post Hoc Year in Review, you listed your positive and negative events and identified commonalities and themes. Determining the themes related to your positive events will encourage you to spend the majority of your time in similar activities, given you are likely to be more productive engaging in work you feel good about, and it feels less like work when participating in projects or experiences that are rooted in your joy or passions (Baker, 2020c).

Once those areas are identified, think about what the intended associated outcomes are and/or can result from those activities that help you advance toward and achieve your intended career goals. In Sarah's case, for example, she spent a great deal of time infusing community-based learning into her courses to both support student learning and contribute to the community she loves so dearly. To be successful in this effort requires a great deal of energy and planning each semester. Walking away from this engagement to free up space for writing and publication preparation was not an option for Sarah, as it would run counter to her values and her engagement as a teacher and community contributor.

Needed Results

My job, as Sarah's academic coach, became helping her think about how she could both leverage this type of pedagogy and passion and turn it into deliverables that would help her work toward full professorship. Collaboratively, we brainstormed how she could make a compelling case for how and why community-based learning is an important pedagogical tool in the humanities. We mapped out two related publications based on her engagement in this space. The first publication was more of a practice piece focused on the model and cognitive framework she employs to support student learning. Her writing provided step-by-step detail about how she envisioned the projects, the learning outcomes associated with the projects, and provided an overview of the assessments she employed, summative and formative to support students' engagement. Her second proposed publication focused on the outcomes of student learning in the humanities. Sarah had a wealth of pre- and post-experience survey data from students who took her courses (seven semesters worth at the time), so we worked to analyze the data and talk through the key findings that related to student learning in the humanities. She targeted pedagogy journals for these manuscripts and presented the model at a professional conference.

Deadlines and Interim Deliverables

Fundamental to any planning process is the establishment of deadlines, including interim deadlines and draft materials. In academe, I suggest soliciting support and engagement from your network of mentors or professional peers for whom you trust and respect. Most of us in the academy do not sit down and write a paper. Rather, we write in stages and the manuscript evolves. Setting up meetings to talk to peers and colleagues in the field as you refine project ideas is useful as is securing friendly reviews on drafts of your work. When you engage these individuals, be sure to establish deadlines for when you will be ready to share ideas and or draft materials for review. Ask them to put those dates on their calendars and ping you as the deadline approaches to help hold you accountable. This also helps you break the work into smaller, manageable pieces to avoid feeling overwhelmed.

Problem Solving

No matter how well laid out a given plan is, life happens. I have many colleagues who prepared thoughtful sabbatical plans and projects they committed to pursue this past year, and those plans were turned upside down because of the pandemic. Here, I offer some quick problem-solving strategies to employ when, as I like to say, "life and work happen."

If a project or effort has veered off course, ask yourself: Why is this project not progressing the way I planned? Consider all the relevant factors, including yourself. Perhaps you are not building in dedicated time on your calendar to do the work needed, or you allow that time to be consumed by others' requests. Alternatively, maybe a co-author is not holding up their responsibility on the work, and they miss deadlines or contribute mediocre work. You need to schedule a meeting to talk about personal and professional accountability to ensure timely progress. Moreover, if that is not possible, it might be time to move on from that collaborator, either temporarily or permanently. Maybe the proposed timeline was just too aggressive, leaving no room for error. Regardless of the reason, you need to identify the issue and work to take corrective action.

Be clear on how you define success in relation to projects, activities, or any other professional or personal endeavor you pursue. Success looks different depending on the project, the person, the context, and the intended recipient. This notion of success is one that I worked hard to adjust, making a shift to internal measures of success as opposed to external measures of success. Granted, that shift is easier to make now that I am a full professor but was critical to feeling successful both personally and professionally. Who cares if I publish another paper if that was at the expense of time with my family, or if I feel professional pressure to attend a weekend work meeting when I should be focused on my kids. My litmus test for success is simple—when my time here is done, will I be on my deathbed thinking to myself, "I really should have attended that Sunday work meeting instead of taking my kids to the park." The answer is "no!" every time, and I feel good with that given I go to bed at night feeling very comfortable with what success means to me and how I measure it.

Chapter Summary and Next Steps

The featured problem in this chapter, **limited dedicated resources and developmental programming aimed at mid-career,** is one that permeates the academy, regardless of institution type. While disappointing, I view this as an opportunity to take control of your own career progression by laying the needed foundation to advance career goals strategically. I realize this type of approach to career advancement may seem unnatural given faculty were not trained in these ways as part of their doctoral studies. However, it becomes necessary to assume agency over your own advancement due to limited formal opportunities for professional growth. One of the most important outcomes of this work is that I not only provide support to those who need it, but they also get "trained" and are better equipped to support those individuals for whom they are tasked with mentoring.

Academics from around the globe are feeling the strain from the pandemic. Higher education's need to respond rapidly was challenging for students, faculty, and staff alike. However, a crucial lesson surfaced in the process—change can happen in higher education, and it can happen quickly. We were forced to innovate to respond to the challenges as we sought to anticipate others that may surface. Those in the academy showed, and continue to show, a great deal of resiliency and nimbleness (an adjective not often associated with higher education). We, in the academy, need to capitalize on that and work to innovate faculty development, specifically for MCF.

The tools, resources, and strategies highlighted are useful whether you are recently tenured and promoted or if you have been at the mid-career stage for a longer period. Regardless at what stage of mid-career you are in, engaging in a Post Hoc Year in Review to assess your successes and growth opportunities is useful to envisioning next steps or informing major professional course corrections. To be successful, you have to be strategic in your own professional investments and consistently employ problem-solving techniques. Looking ahead to Chapter 3, I will help you use your departmental and institutional strategic priorities as a framework for organizing and communicating your highlight reel.

References

AAUP (American Association of University Professors) (2014). Contingent appointments and the academic profession. *AAUP*. www.aaup.org/file/Contingent%20Appointment.pdf

Baker, V. L., Pifer, M. J., & Lunsford, L. G. (2016). Faculty challenges across rank in liberal arts colleges: A human resources perspective. *The Journal of Faculty Development*, 30(1), 23–30.

Baker, V. L., Lunsford, L. G., & Pifer, M. J. (2017). *Developing faculty in liberal arts colleges: Aligning individual needs and organizational goals*. Rutgers University Press.

Baker, V. L., Pifer, M. J., & Lunsford, L. G. (2018). Faculty development in liberal arts colleges: A look at divisional trends, preferences, and needs. *Higher Education Research & Development*, 37(7), 1336–1351.

Baker, V. L. (2020a, March 25). How colleges can better help faculty during the pandemic. *Inside HigherEd*. www.insidehighered.com/views/2020/03/25/recommendations-how-colleges-can-better-support-their-faculty-during-covid-19

Baker, V. L. (2020b, September 8). Now's not the time to cut faculty development funds. *Inside HigherEd*. www.insidehighered.com/advice/2020/09/08/four-ways-investing-professional-development-now-can-benefit-both-faculty-and

Baker, V. L. (2020c). *Charting your path to full: A Guide for women associate professors*. Rutgers University Press.

Baker, V. L., & Manning, C. E. (2021). A mid-career faculty agenda: A review of four decades of research and practice. *Higher Education: Handbook of Theory and Research: Volume 36*, 1–66.Bouchrika, I. (2020). 11 top trends in higher education: 2020/2021 data, insights, & predictions. *Guide2Research*. www.guide2research.com/research/trends-in-higher-education

Collins, J. (2001). *Good to great*. New York: Harper Collins.

Espinosa, L. L., Turk, J. M., Taylor, M., & Chessman, H. M. (2019). Race and ethnicity in higher education: A status report. *American Council of Education*. Washington DC. https://tacc.org/sites/default/files/documents/2019-03/race-and-ethnicity-in-higher-education.pdf

Feldman, D. C., & Turnley, W. H. (2001). A field study of adjunct faculty: The impact of career stage on reactions to non-tenure-track jobs. *Journal of Career Development, 28*(1), 1–16.

Flaherty, C. (2018, October 12). A non-tenure track profession? *Inside HigherEd.* www.insidehighered.com/news/2018/10/12/about-three-quarters-all-faculty-positions-are-tenure-track-according-new-aaup#:~:text=Part%2Dtime%20faculty%20positions%20increased,time%2C%20tenure%2Dtrack%20professors.

Hurlburt, S., & McGarrah, M. (2016). The shifting academic workforce: Where are the contingent faculty. *Delta Cost Project at American Institutes for Research.* www. air.org/sites/default/files/downloads/report/Shifting-Academic-Workforce-November-2016. pdf.

Kezar, A. (2012). Spanning the great divide between tenure-track and non-tenure-track faculty. *Change: The Magazine of Higher Learning, 44*(6), 6–13.

Kezar, A., Holcombe, E., & Maxey, D. (2016). Rethinking faculty models/ roles: An emerging consensus about future directions for the professoriate. *TIAA Institute.* www.tiaainstitute.org/publication/rethinking-faculty-models roles.

Mathews, K. R. (2014). Perspectives on midcareer faculty and advice for supporting them. *The Collaborative on Academic Careers in Higher Education.* https://coache.gse.harvard.edu/files/gse-coache/files/coache-perspectives-on.pdf?m=1447625224

National Center for Education Statistics (2018). U.S. Department of Education. Institute of Education Sciences, National Center for Education Statistics. https://nces.ed.gov/fastfacts/display.asp?id=61

Pew Charitable Trust (2019). Two decades of change in federal and state higher education funding. www.pewtrusts.org/-/media/assets/2019/10/fedstatefundinghigheredu_chartbook_v1.pdf

Polikoff, M., Silver, D., & Korn, S. (2020, August 4). What's the likely impact of COVID-19 on higher Ed? *Inside HigherEd.* www.insidehighered.com/views/2020/08/04/analysis-data-national-survey-impact-pandemic-higher-ed-opinion

Snyder, T. D. (1993). *120 years of American education: A statistical portrait.* U.S. Department of Education. Office of Educational Research and Improvement. National Center for Education Statistics.

St. Amour, M. (2020, October 15). Report: Enrollment continues to trend down. *Inside HigherEd.* www.insidehighered.com/news/2020/10/15/worrying-enrollment-trends-continue-clearinghouse-report-shows

Vedder, R. (2017, August 25). Universities: Then and now. *Forbes.* www.forbes.com/sites/ccap/2017/08/25/universities-then-and-now/?sh=645662717c19

Waltman, J., Bergom, I., Hollenshead, C., Miller, J., & August, L. (2012). Factors contributing to job satisfaction and dissatisfaction among non-tenure-track faculty. *The Journal of Higher Education, 83*(3), 411–434.

Wiley (2021, February 1). Top challenges facing U.S. higher education. *Wiley Education Services.* https://edservices.wiley.com/top-higher-education-challenges/

Yakoboski, P. J. (2015, May). The career experience of academics in adjunct faculty positions. *TIAA Institute.* www.tiaainstitute.org/sites/default/files/presentations/2017-02/adjunct_career_experience_full.pdf

Chapter 3

Turning Promotion Guidelines and Strategic Imperatives into an Organizing Framework

Ashley, a faculty member in the fine and applied arts at a research university, has the goal of full professorship in sight, but she has some serious concerns about the process to get there. Ashley has been deliberate in her approach, putting the pieces of her dossier together over the past year. In her words, "I believe I am in pretty good shape, but there seem to be various unknowns ahead especially due to COVID-19 and the university's significant budget cuts." The notion of tenure and the merits of tenure are on the line at Ashley's institution, and this is causing all faculty there to have serious concerns about their futures at the institution should tenure be abolished. Those who are fully immersed in tenure and promotion processes currently, like Ashley, are doubly concerned wondering if they will even be reviewed. Ashley is frustrated about several points. First, it is not clear to her if the university plans to freeze the process this year simply to "save money." As Ashley stated, "I hate to invest this time and energy when it is not clear when and how we will know if reviews for tenure and promotion will be a 'go' or not." Her second concern is about related processes, specifically the role of external reviews and how those reviewers will be secured. In the past at Ashley's institution, a list of possible external reviewers was compiled in March/April, and either a university or departmental representative approached potential reviewers in May/June. However, as Ashley shared, "I heard from my colleagues at other institutions that their requests last year were turned down quite a bit even though they approached in May. The reason for the turning down was that those individuals who were approached had already committed to other P&T or full reviews." All of these unknowns caused Ashley to wonder—What can I or the university do about this? Finally, Ashley is hearing mixed advice about her role with

DOI: 10.4324/9781003201311-5

possible external reviews. She said, "I heard that some faculty approach potential reviewers in advance to give a heads up; whereas others think it's unethical. I personally do not know what is appropriate here."

The fear of the unknown can be quite crippling. Unfortunately, the general unknowns that Ashley has identified are not unique to her situation or institution. Most certainly, the COVID-19 pandemic and the future role of tenure at her institution has added to the concerns at both the faculty and institutional levels. However, many of Ashley's concerns stem from a lack of clarity related to her institution's advancement to full processes. Ashley should have the knowledge needed to advance should she aspire to do so. Being ill-prepared (e.g., materials are unorganized) or not ready (e.g., unfulfilled advancement criteria) to achieve full professorship are entirely different issues compared to lacking the understanding or knowledge to adequately prepare for this professional hurdle or to advance toward other professional goals. Ashley's experience epitomizes the featured problem in this chapter: **Inadequate guidance on how to advance toward professional (and personal) goals.**

The concerns and fears that Ashley has identified are real and valid, and many of them are also avoidable. I once again want to remind you, the reader, that it is imperative for you to exert agency over your own goals and aspirations. I was recently a panelist with three other accomplished women, representing various career stages, industries, and professional titles. A startup tech firm hosted the panel, which focused on women supporting women on their career journeys. One of the panelists communicated that is it not up to your organization or institution to manage your career—that is your job. However, she expressed that organizations and institutions *do* have a responsibility to provide their employees with the resources and knowledge needed to advance along their professional journeys.

In this chapter, I discuss the most common knowledge barriers mid-career faculty (MCF) face as they consider advancement to full, as well as other barriers to career advancement. I return to Ashley's experience to think about and propose steps Ashley can take to increase her knowledge. Finally, I provide you with a career progression framework to help you manage your career goals and aspirations. To undergird the career progression framework, I walk you through how to build in evaluation criteria and your institutional (and departmental) strategic priorities.

What Do You Need to Know?

As I shared in Chapter 2, in order to play the game, you need to know the rules. Throughout my faculty development and consulting engagements,

I have been astounded at the number of faculty members, regardless of institution type and discipline, who confide that they are not clear on what it takes, in terms of both content *and* process, to advance to full professorship or other advanced career opportunities at their respective institutions. This knowledge is fundamental to being informed and strategic about pursuing your career goals (Baker, 2020). Blain (2020) wrote, "For those of us who are deeply committed to transforming the academy—even as we recognize its many limitations and challenges— becoming a full professor is an important step" (para 4). A step, I believe, that should be supported with clear metrics and processes.

As Freeman and colleagues (2020) noted, "…the absence of clear guidelines for promotion to a full professorship can leave associate professors in a vulnerable position, particularly faculty who have been in the rank of associate for an extended period of time" (p. 2). Lack of know-ledge relates to three key factors: (a) lack of clarity in terms of evaluation criteria; (b) lack of clarity in terms of process (e.g., time, who is involved, what materials are required); and (c) lack of understanding about the outcome(s) of earning full professor (e.g., what does full professorship "get me") (Baker, 2020). Choosing to not advance to full professorship is one thing; not advancing because the path to achieve full professor-ship is unclear is an entirely different issue. In this section, I discuss the three predominant factors that impede progress to full professorship, as well as highlight the institutional biases women and underrepresented faculty populations face along this journey.

Lack of Clarity on Evaluation Criteria

For those on the tenure track, there is likely nothing more vital than understanding the metrics or criteria by which you will be evaluated. Traditionally, these criteria relate to the triumvirate that characterizes the academy—teaching, research, and service. Institutions weigh these areas differently based on mission and institutional priorities. Other evaluation categories I have seen included are contribution to community (campus and surrounding), mentoring, leadership, and reputation in the field (domestic, international).

How evaluation criteria are defined and acted upon differ based on a variety of factors such as institutional mission and division. Despite these differences, the goal (and hope) is to provide adequate guidance to faculty, and personnel committees who review application materials, while leaving room to display the unique paths faculty members pursue in the academy. Recently scholars examined promotion guidelines at 134 institutions classified as R2: doctoral universities with high research activity (Freeman et al., 2020). The authors argued that without trans-parent language, MCF might become stagnant or stalled. Based on their review of institutional language and policy, only 38 universities out of the 134 examined provided some general information "with few specifics and/or distinctions for the promotion to full professor" (p. 7). Thirty-four of the identified 38 institutions "provided vague, yet high expectations around teaching, service, leadership, and/or research without any explicit requirements…" (Freeman et al., 2020, p. 7). While this review targeted research universities, these same issues surface to varying degrees across institutions, domestically and abroad (Demetry & Lingo, 2019; Subbaye, 2017; Subbaye & Vithal, 2017).

No doubt, there is a tension between providing specific guidance without becoming too rigid, thus removing opportunities to highlight the diverse ways faculty engage in their careers. Legal considerations are also at play at the departmental and institutional levels. However, as someone who teaches human resources, I am a big fan of realistic job previews. By communicating the good and bad characteristics of a job, job expectations are re-established for existing employees (Tucker, 2012). Just as faculty are expected to develop over the span of their careers, so too should evaluation criteria to account for the growth and maturity that happens as faculty members evolve as teachers, scholars, and community contributors.

Lack of Clarity on Process

In addition to lack of clarity related to evaluation criteria, the process by which promotion decisions are determined is also murky for many faculty seeking to advance to full. Returning to research by Freeman and colleagues (2020), of the 38 institutions identified only 12 (32%) of those institutions "incorporated explicit procedural steps along with expectations for the promotion to full professor" (p. 7). They further observed, "The procedural steps for the promotion to full professor included but were not limited to the personnel or committees involved, the timeline, and/or the application or documents required" (p. 7). Documenting and communicating this information is fundamental and necessary knowledge to ensure faculty who seek full professorship are prepared to do so.

Compounding the problem is many faculty are unsure of *where* to locate the needed information, if available. Faculty handbooks are a good first place to start, but there is potential for several "keepers" to manage the necessary information. Freeman and colleagues' (2020) study revealed five key entities that housed promotion to full information that included the office of the provost, office of the president, faculty senate, human resources, and a specific college/school. I vividly remember conducting an MCF focus group in which I asked about their experiences, goals, and needed supports (Baker et al., 2017). During the focus group, a faculty colleague noted concerns about the evaluation process, lamenting the lack of information on their college's website. She further elaborated on the confusing nature of what was included. The other four colleagues in that faculty focus group looked somewhat surprised, and expressed dismay and slight embarrassment about not knowing this information was even available. Their colleague replied, "I only found it by accident."

Assuming agency over this process is necessary to success. As I shared earlier in the chapter, it is not your institution's responsibility to manage your career; it is yours. Nevertheless, it is disappointing when institutions fail to fulfill *their* responsibility, which is to provide the foundational information needed to enable faculty who aspire to full to understand the associated expectations and the processes by which those expectations are realized. Yet, I know from my own research and that of others, campus leaders and administrators believe investing in MCF is important (Baker et al., 2017; Baker et al., 2016). "As deans, provosts, and presidents will tell you, the question of how best to support associate professors is on the radar, widely known as something our institutions do not do well" (Dever & Justice, 2021, para 2).

What Does Earning Full Professorship Get Me?

Overcoming knowledge barriers is vital to advancing toward full professorship or any other advanced career aspiration. However, another sticking point I hear frequently is the cost-benefit analysis of advancing to full. Make no mistake, that journey requires discipline, sacrifice, support, and understanding. Many faculty colleagues question the need to advance given the personal and professional sacrifices required to get there, not to mention the well-documented institutional barriers, which make advancement challenging (Ward & Wolf-Wendel, 2012). I would be remiss if I did not highlight the very real question that arises for MCF as they consider their next career move—what does earning full professorship get me?

I agree with Blain's (2020) assessment, "...promotion to full professor is not simply about individual success. It is about the ability to harness institutional power and influence to help open doors and create opportunities for people who might otherwise be shut out" (para 4). However, the lack of clarity and understanding about how this process works, and what and who is involved, minimizes the possible benefits. The question of "is it worth it?" has implications beyond the individual; that question should be a wakeup call for everyone in the academy.

Barriers toward Advancement

Finally, it is also important to draw attention to the institutional biases and barriers that impede career advancement for select populations of faculty, particularly women and underrepresented faculty populations (Baker, 2020; Blain, 2020; Croom, 2017; Hart, 2016; Ward & Wolf-Wendel, 2012). Women and faculty of color advance to full professor at a slower rate compared to their White male counterparts (Colby & Fowler, 2020). Some argue that is because of higher standards and expectations of performance placed on these populations of faculty (Matthew, 2016). Scholars point to ideal and gendered worker norms, which still dominate the academy (Hart, 2016). Further, how the academy defines productivity and determines where productivity happens still disproportionately benefits men (Baker, 2021).

I was recently on a Zoom call with a group of colleagues. Several of my male colleagues were clearly joining the meeting from home. However, the provost (who is male) commented to a female colleague that it was nice to see her joining the meeting from her office. Microaggressions like this still happen every day and send a signal about what is and is not valued while simultaneously highlighting a pervasive double standard. Couple these microaggressions with ill-defined promotion criteria and processes, and it is no wonder why women and faculty of color advance at slower rates, if at all, to full professorship. Not surprisingly, their pay also lags behind (Weissman, 2020). Strategy and planning is especially beneficial in order to manage these realities.

Advancing to full professorship or any other career goal is a choice that some faculty members opt to pursue for a variety of reasons. To be successful, one must be clear about the goal and commit to doing the work needed to achieve that goal. However, being informed and equipped with the needed knowledge to achieve those goals is fundamental. Institutional and departmental processes have room for improvement as evidenced from the information shared in this section. However, the focus of this chapter is offering you the needed tools and resources to take control of the process by educating yourself and guiding you in your efforts.

Returning to Ashley's Experience

Ashley's experience featured in the opening of the chapter occurs in a contentious institutional environment, which adds to the anxiety of the promotion processes. I want to note that Ashley is not a client of mine, but rather I met Ashley while attending a workshop I led at her institution. A group of faculty at her institution read *Charting Your Path to Full*, and I was invited to help MCF work through the tools and resources featured in the book. Prior to the workshop, I reached out to registered participants to inquire about their biggest areas of need to inform our time together. Ashley connected with me and shared the concerns featured in the opening case. That sparked an email correspondence with Ashley and between institutional leaders on her campus and myself.

Revisit Ashley's experience at the beginning of this chapter and record your reactions. What questions arise for you? How would you help Ashley, and what advice would you offer? Write down your thoughts and observations in the space provided. Next, we will work through her situation together.

_____

_____

_____

_____

_____

_____

_____

_____

_____

_____

_____

_____

_____

_____

_____

_____

_____

_____

_____

_____

_____

Relevant Facts

There is a great deal to unpack in Ashley's scenario; many conflicting issues merge to create a challenging situation. Not surprising, the pandemic is playing a role in promotion considerations at the institutional and individual levels. Budget cuts are a concern across all of higher education. Yet, they are manifesting in different ways. At Ashley's institution, the budget issues are causing institutional leaders across the state to ponder the value of tenure, which Ashley needs help managing given she is immersed in preparing her dossier for full consideration.

Based on what has been communicated at the institutional level, it is unclear if the budget cuts will affect the present year's P&T review processes. Preparing promotion materials is a time-intensive activity, and Ashley lacks the needed knowledge to make an informed decision about how much, if any, time to invest preparing this year. In addition, there are unclear process-related issues, namely the role of external reviews. Ashley has a lack of clarity about how external reviewers are contacted, who is responsible for contacting them, and the timing of those invitations. She has also received mixed feedback on how much involvement she should, or should not have, in the process, which is triggering ethical concerns for her.

Key Stakeholders

The primary stakeholder mentioned in Ashley's case is the institution. Based on her email response to my initial inquiry, Ashley struggles with how to move forward or identifying whom to reach out to for help. I certainly appreciated Ashley's confidence in me, as someone who could help her navigate these challenges. However, I also found it problematic that at least based on the information provided in the initial email, Ashley did not feel comfortable asking these questions to someone at her institution. Lack of explicit communication related to budget cuts and the impact those cuts would or could have on P&T processes and decisions was at the core of Ashley's issues.

Needed Information

Once I read Ashley's email, I sprang into action to better educate myself on the institutional challenges and related concerns. If Ashley was having these concerns, other workshop attendees were likely to be in a similar situation. First, I needed to learn more about the institutional budget cuts and the associated conversations that were happening about tenure across the state and at the institution. One of Ashley's peers also emailed me and shared the challenges related to tenure and kindly included links to several news articles that helped me gain a bigger picture of the issue and where the matter stood presently.

I reached out to my institutional contacts and shared excerpts of Ashley's email with them, without revealing her identity. I asked them if they could provide insight into the questions, specifically if it was worthwhile for candidates to continue pursuing tenure and/or promotion in spite of the budget cuts. I also sought to gain clarity on who is responsible for securing external reviewers and any associated strategies for ensuring external reviewers accept the invitation.

One of my institutional contacts reached out and suggested a phone call to talk through the larger institutional/environmental issues to give me needed background. She, along with another colleague, provided insight into the specific questions and assured me P&T reviews were still happening this year despite budget cuts, and that department chairs should be taking the lead on reaching out to and securing external reviewers. Fortunately, I was able to communicate this information to Ashley and offer some related advice as she prepares her materials.

Case Summary

Advancing toward any career goal, whether it be full professorship or a senior leadership position, can be anxiety-inducing even for the most prepared individual. The pandemic and associated implications only add to the unknowns. The pandemic exacerbated the lack of process clarity in Ashley's case, and she did not feel comfortable reaching out to peers at her institution to secure the needed guidance. My guess is she would have felt more comfortable having a face-to-face conversation to ask these questions but the remote work arrangement did not allow that to happen, which only highlights how informal and peer learning aids career development. Ashley needed a trusted network of individuals for support. No doubt impression management was at play, given I was able to secure the needed information from my institutional contacts, which I shared with Ashley. Fortunately, I have long-term relationships with both contacts, well known as faculty advocates at their institutions and in the field of higher education. In the next section, I walk you through a career progression framework to help you organize your dossier materials or to help advance toward other professional goals. The following framework serves as a tool to organize your plans and as a visual summary of your progress.

Tools, Strategies, and Resources

While not every human resources tool or strategy from industry is applicable or useful in higher education, I do believe some tools, with adjustments, can provide a value add. One such approach to career development that I believe has a great deal of merit is a career progression framework given it accounts for career stages and growth opportunities (Heathfield, 2019). A career progression framework keeps employees engaged and demonstrates an organizational commitment. Such a framework provides a visual snapshot of where employees currently stand, provides a pathway toward advancement, and fosters ownership for advancing along the career pathway. When employed organizationally, such a framework also facilitates a consistent approach to promotions, leading to greater equity and a sense of fairness (NOBL Academy, 2020). In this section, I offer an example of a career progression framework that employs my PSEI (Purpose, Scope, Evidence of Impact) model for organizing and communicating your contributions.

Career Progression Framework

Whether you are new to mid-career or are a seasoned veteran, it is imperative to have a plan and an organizational framework to help you engage in a regular self-assessment about your progress in relation to that plan. A career progression framework can be a valuable tool that helps you achieve these aims. I am a big fan of planning in three- to five-year increments; therefore, I organized the framework according to a three-year runway. Organize the framework and corresponding parameters in a way that feels comfortable to you. Note, be sure to incorporate planned life moments (e.g., family planning, assuming an administrative role) so you can build your approach around these important personal and professional moments.

Grab a pen/pencil and use the space provided to jot down your initial thoughts on the following six steps:

STEP 1. ESTABLISH GOALS

Before you can embark on any career planning, you need to be clear about what you are seeking to achieve. This goal is at the core of the career progression planning.

STEP 2. IDENTIFY RESOURCES IN HAND

Organize and create an inventory (e.g., a bulleted list) of the resources you have in hand to achieve your goals. Some items to consider include your mentors, knowledge of related processes (e.g., promotion criteria and process-related information), and career development supports at your institution or professional association (e.g., training workshops).

STEP 3. TARGET RESOURCES NEEDED

Maybe you need more time blocked off in your schedule to achieve your goals, or perhaps you need a mentor with a particular skill set or experience to guide you. Whatever your needs are, be sure to note this information, along with an explicit plan of how you will acquire those resources.

STEP 4. CREATE A TIMELINE

Be explicit about the runway you have ahead in terms of goal achievement. If your goal is full professorship and you are new to mid-career, you likely have five to seven years to prepare. If you are a seasoned MCF member, you may have a shorter runway with which to work.

STEP 5. ANTICIPATE ROADBLOCKS

No matter how much you plan, organize, and prepare, life happens. Think through the possible roadblocks or hurdles that may arise that might impede your progress. Make a note about how you plan to manage those roadblocks should they arise.

STEP 6. DESIGN ACCOUNTABILITY MEASURES

Lastly, holding yourself accountable is vital to your success. Be explicit about how you plan to hold yourself accountable. Perhaps these measures include self-imposed deadlines and peer accountability. Whatever you employ, be explicit about it.

Now that you have written your preliminary thoughts, let's start filling out your career progression framework.

What to Include

In addition to your notes from the six steps, obtain available departmental and/or institutional evaluation criteria and institutional strategic priorities. All of this information will inform your career progression framework. The example I include is based on my advancement to full professorship goal. My advice is to create a separate framework for each of the criteria for which you will be evaluated. As I work through my goals and related plans, I like to scaffold my approach. This means, note your goal (e.g., skills and competencies you hope to develop), your plan for achieving the goal, and the explicit activities you will engage in to support your growth throughout the process (See Table 3.1). Also, be sure to note resources in hand and resources needed to achieve the plans you outline in your career progression framework.

I also recommend including an outcomes column where you can document the evidence of your engagement. This is where the PSEI approach comes into play. In my previous book (Baker, 2020), I introduced the notion of Purpose (P) and Scope (S) as a way of communicating your professional engagement and reach. I define purpose as the "reason behind a given activity and the associated goal of that activity" (p. 73). Scope refers to "the depth and breadth that a given effort spans, including details about the beneficiary" (p. 73). I expand on that approach here to include Evidence of Impact (EI), which I define as the contribution and/or measurable outcome of your engagement (including the impact your engagement has on you professionally and personally).

Career Progression Example

To demonstrate the career progression framework in action, I will share how I used the six steps to achieve my professional goal of gaining more experience in large-scale research projects as I worked toward full professorship. I wanted to illustrate my ability to lead a research team and to enhance my quantitative and qualitative analysis skill sets. I also wanted to advance my reputation in the field of faculty development in general, with a specific emphasis in liberal arts colleges. I have always worked to ensure my research informs practice, because I am not interested in engaging in research for the sake of research. Rather, I seek to take knowledge gleaned from my research to improve the lives and experiences of those individuals for whom I am most focused. I organize my discussion using the PSEI approach.

I, along with two amazing colleagues, launched the Initiative for Faculty Development in Liberal Arts Colleges (Baker et al., 2017) to learn more about the faculty experience in liberal arts colleges, an understudied institutional setting, and to ultimately inform the development of resources and tools that would support faculty as they advanced along their career. A sub-project of this effort (noted in Year 2 of Table 3.1) was an initiative titled, Supporting Mid-career Faculty Members. The Purpose (P) of that project was to identify challenges MCF face and the needed supports in the Great Lakes Colleges Association (GLCA). In terms of Scope (S), to ensure our efforts would have the intended reach, we engaged in a mixed-methods study. Our research included focus groups at four of the GLCA member institutions, a survey administration across all 13 member institutions, and follow-up interviews with MCF who self-selected as part of the survey administration. Areas covered in this research included career stage challenges, institutional supports, leadership aspirations/experiences, P&T, and work/personal considerations.

An outcome (Evidence of Impact—EI) of this work was the development and delivery of the Academic Leadership Institute (ALI) (Baker et al., 2019) for MCF, which we delivered for the GLCA. The ALI was funded by the Henry Luce Foundation in New York City. This scholarly effort produced a variety of outcomes, including publications, presentations, and the ALI. In my narrative for full, I highlighted the EI across these deliverables, including the comments from ALI attendees about the impact their engagement had on their own career progression. I also talked about how my involvement in this initiative informed my evolution as a scholar and practitioner.

If you are like me, you pursue projects because they bring you joy and ultimately help you achieve your intended career contribution. As MCF engage in their work, it is not always clear how, or in what ways, these intended contributions affect others. Recently, I received the loveliest email from a past ALI participant, who shared the following:

Dear Vicki,

I hope things are going well during this crazy time. I attended Lead Mentor Develop several years ago now so you may not remember me. I think I had just been made dept chair (which I was angry about because I found it hard to stay research active) when I attended. I took that though and ran with it and went from Department chair to Division Chair and now I am going up for full professor. I managed to get back into research and publishing too; everything fell in line and I am even working on a nice grant now. As we close on this, the strangest of semesters, I wanted to let you know your program made a big difference for me. Thank you.

This faculty member participated in the program during the 2016–2017 academic year, and I appreciated hearing about his progress all these years later.

Table 3.1 Career Progression Template—Scholarly Development (Evaluation Criteria)

Year 1	Outcomes	Institutional Priority/Strategic Imperative	Year 2	Outcomes	Institutional Priority/Strategic Imperative	Year 3	Outcomes	Institutional Priority/Strategic Imperative
Exhibit ability to lead a large-scale research project	P: S: EI:		1. Advance a research agenda 2. Become subject matter expert on my campus	P: S: EI:	Focus on the intentional integration of knowledge	Turn research into practice	P: S: EI:	Focus on the intentional integration of knowledge
1. Connect with GLCA consortium 2. Apply for internal and external funding	P: S: EI:	1. Forge sustainable local/global partnerships 2. Exercise effective stewardship of all resources	1. Further foster critical relationship 2. Leverage consortial opportunities	P: S: EI:		Develop programming for an Academic Leadership Institute (ALI), targeted at mid-career	P: S: EI:	1. Forge sustainable local/global partnerships 2. Build an open, diverse, and inclusive college community (focused on consortial level)

	P: S: EI:	P: S: EI:	P: S: EI:	P: S: EI:
Related projects or scholarly engagement	1. Launch IFDLAC study 2. Build on early career faculty research and practice	1. Pursue sub-project focused on MCF 2. Disseminate findings to GLCA Deans, inform practice on campuses	1. Forge sustainable local/global partnerships 2. Build an open, diverse, and inclusive college community	1. Launch first ALI for GLCA 2. Publish papers on research findings and model of ALI
Resources in Hand	1. Faculty Development Committee 2. Grants coordinator	1. Relationship with GLA 2. Internal grant funds		1. Consortial support 2. External grant funds
Resources Needed	Support of GLCA President, 13 Academic Deans	1. Support securing external funding		

1. Exercise effective stewardship of all resources 2. Focus on the intentional integration of knowledge

Strategic Priorities

In addition to being clear about the Purpose and Scope of a given activity, accompanied by the Evidence of Impact, you must connect your engagement to your departmental and/or institutional priorities, if the connection exists. Note, a column in Table 3.1 is specifically for this purpose. The information you see in these columns is based on the four strategic pillars that were drivers at Albion College at the time I was advancing to full professorship. The pillars were: Focus on the Intentional Integration of Knowledge; Build an Open, Diverse, and Inclusive College Community; Forge Sustainable Local Partnerships and Global Collaborations; and Exercise Effective Stewardship of all Resources. My goal was to illustrate for the personnel committee that my engagement in these scholarly activities not only supported my professional growth but was also in service to the institution, aimed at helping it achieve the ideals and values set forth during strategic planning under the direction of that administration.

My (and my colleagues') engagement in this work helped to create a community of MCF across the GLCA consortium, a community I am still very proud of and active in fostering (Pillar Three—Forge Sustainable Local Partnerships and Global Collaborations). I discussed how critical this community is to faculty in liberal arts colleges given we are often isolated in scholarly areas. In Table 3.1, I point to explicit examples of how my work supports the institutional goal of intentional integration of knowledge (Pillar One) given my research and practice would support faculty at Albion College as they advanced in their careers. The human resource lessons learned would benefit and serve as examples of career development and leadership challenges that I could share in my under-graduate courses; the ALI was an example of how data can and should inform program development aimed at better supporting mid-career professionals.

Given our research included all MCF across the GLCA, we learned about the experiences and needs of specific populations of faculty (e.g., women, faculty of color, LGBTQ). This allowed us to target our related communications to the GLCA deans about the needs of these faculty populations. We offered suggestions on how to better support diverse faculty (Pillar Two—Build an Open, Diverse, and Inclusive College Community), and I shared the findings with Albion College's Faculty Committee on Diversity to inform institutional practices and policy moving forward.

In sum, advancing toward any goal requires focus, a strategy, and plans to execute your strategy effectively. The career progression frame-work requires you to articulate your goals, explicitly state the plan(s) you will pursue to get there, and help you identify the activities you need to engage in to arrive at your intended destination. You must also be thoughtful about resources in hand, and resources needed to be successful.

Be mindful and purposeful as you populate your own career progression framework and employ the PSEI approach. As you prepare your narrative and share examples of your work across your institutional evaluation criteria, be sure to clearly articulate the driving Purpose behind your engagement, the Scope your engagement spans, and include Evidence of Impact for the intended stakeholders (and for yourself). Be explicit about linking your engagement to institutional (or departmental) strategic priorities. Communicate how your work helps you grow and develop as a professional but also how your work is in service to the broader departmental and institutional mission and priorities.

Chapter Summary and Next Steps

I think all of us aspire to advance in our careers, and that advancement can take many forms at various stages throughout the life cycle of our professional journey. Yet, it becomes quite challenging to advance without having clear goals and the needed support to facilitate success along the way. Being in mid-career does not mean we have all the answers. In fact, quite the opposite is true. Yet, the academy is notorious for providing **inadequate guidance on how to advance toward professional (and personal) goals,** the featured problem in this chapter.

As you progress in your academic career, what is needed to get to your final destination becomes somewhat more complicated given all the moving parts and pieces MCF are expected to manage simultaneously. I urge you to be precise about your goals; one cannot underestimate the importance of a clearly articulated strategy, plans to execute your strategy, and built-in accountability measures, both personal and external, to ensure you progress in a timely manner.

The career progression framework, along with the PSEI approach, is a tool that can help you assume agency over your career progression. You now have a roadmap to identify action steps to pursue, activities in which to engage, and clarity on what you have and need to move forward. You can, and should, leverage your evaluation criteria and institutional (and departmental) strategic priorities to ground your work and contributions so involved stakeholders are clear on your value add. In Chapter 4, the final chapter of Part 1, we hone in on the importance of executing your plans as you seek to advance in your career.

References

Baker, V. L., Pifer, M. J., & Lunsford, L. G. (2016). Faculty challenges across rank in liberal arts colleges: A human resources perspective. *The Journal of Faculty Development*, 30(1), 23–30.

Baker, V. L., Lunsford, L. G., & Pifer, M. J. (2017). *Developing faculty in liberal arts colleges: Aligning individual needs and organizational goals*. Rutgers University Press.

Baker, V. L., Lunsford, L. G., & Pifer, M. J. (2019). The academic leadership institute for mid-career faculty. In V. L. Baker, L. G. Lunsford, G. Neisler, A. L. Terosky, & M. J. Pifer (Eds.), *Success after tenure: Supporting mid-career faculty* (pp. 35–54). Stylus Publishing.

Baker, V. L. (2020). *Charting your path to full: A guide for women associate professors*. Rutgers University Press.

Baker, V. L. (2021). Women in higher education: Re-imagining leadership in the academy in times of crisis. *Journal of Faculty Development*, 35(1), 57–62.

Blain, K. N. (2020, May 22). From associate to full. *Inside HigherEd*. www.insidehighered.com/advice/2020/05/22/guidance-how-move-associate-full-professor-opinion

Colby, G., & Fowler, C. (2020, December 9). Data snapshot looks at full-time women faculty and faculty of color. *Academe Blog*. https://academeblog.org/2020/12/09/data-snapshot-looks-at-full-time-women-faculty-and-faculty-of-color/

Croom, N. N. (2017). Promotion beyond tenure: Unpacking racism and sexism in the experiences of Black womyn professors. *The Review of Higher Education*, 40(4), 557–583.

Demetry, C., & Lingo, E. L. (2019, January). Transforming the associate-to-full promotion system: Wrestling with strategic ambiguity and gender equity. *ASEE annual conference proceedings*. www.asee.org/public/conferences/140/papers/25497/view

Dever, C., & Justice, G. (2021, February 3). How to avoid the associate-professor trap. *The Chronicle of Higher Education*. www.chronicle.com/article/how-to-avoid-the-associate-professor-trap?cid2=gen_login_refresh&cid=gen_sign_in

Freeman, S., Douglas, T. & Goodenough, T. (2020). Toward best practices for promotion to full professor guidelines at research universities. *eJournal of Education Policy*, 21(2). https://doi.org/10.37803/ejepF2004

Hart, J. (2016). Dissecting a gendered organization: Implications for career trajectories for mid-career faculty women in STEM. *The Journal of Higher Education*, 87(5), 605–634.

Heathfield, S. M. (2019, November 3). Steps to create a career development plan. *The Balance Careers*. www.thebalancecareers.com/steps-to-create-a-career-development-plan-1917798

Matthew, P. A. (Ed.). (2016). *Written/unwritten: Diversity and the hidden truths of tenure*. UNC Press Books.

NOBL Academy. (2020, October 16). What to watch out for when designing career development frameworks. https://academy.nobl.io/what-to-watch-out-for-when-designing-career-development-frameworks/#:~:text=Establishing%20a%20career%20progression%20framework,how%20they%20want%20to%20grow

Subbaye, R. (2017). The shrinking professoriate: Academic promotion and university teaching. *South African Journal of Higher Education, 31*(3), 249–273.

Subbaye, R., & Vithal, R. (2017). Teaching criteria that matter in university academic promotions. *Assessment & Evaluation in Higher Education, 42*(1), 37–60.

Tucker, M. A. (2012, January 1). Show and tell. *HR Magazine.* www.shrm.org/hr-today/news/hr-magazine/pages/0112tucker.aspx

Ward, K., & Wolf-Wendel, L. (2012). *Academic motherhood: How faculty manage work and family.* Rutgers University Press.

Weissman, S. (2020, December 17). Female faculty continue to face stubborn wage gap and underrepresentation in tenured positions. *Diverse Issues in Higher Education.* https://diverseeducation.com/article/199634/

Chapter 4

Executing Your Plans

Brad is a STEM faculty member at a regional comprehensive university. Brad is also a faculty of color. He has been planning to advance to full for four-and-a-half years and feels confident that they are "the right" plans to achieve his goals. First, he aims to earn full professorship (goal #1) as a necessary credential to become a dean (goal #2) on his respective campus. He loves the academic side of his life but wants to expand on his experience as department chair, a role he relished given it allowed him to engage with colleagues and other departments and units across campus in "new and exciting ways." While Brad believed he was moving in the right direction, he felt "blindsided" by a conversation with his department chair about his prospects for full professorship. Brad thought he would submit his dossier in two years, but his department chair thinks he has a better likelihood of being successful submitting in three to four years. That timeframe means Brad will miss applying for the dean role when it reopens and will have to wait another cycle. This interaction caused Brad to both question his long-term goals and interest in staying in the academy. After reflecting on that meeting, Brad reached out to his trusted colleague in a different department on campus to review his plans to achieve full professorship and help ensure he is competitive for the deanship. After review, Brad's peer shared the same feedback that his department chair did. His peer felt that Brad was clear about his goals and laid out some solid short and long term plans to achieve those goals. Where Brad fell short, however, was in the execution of those plans. When pressed to illustrate evidence of progress, Brad struggled to do so. He realized that he needed help executing his plans effectively to ensure he could achieve his goals in the desired timeframe. It was time for Brad to recalibrate.

DOI: 10.4324/9781003201311-6

In the past few chapters, you have identified your goal(s) and articulated short- and long-term plans to achieve those goals. Yet, you might be falling short in advancing at the pace or in the ways, you intended. This is a common phenomenon at the organizational and individual levels. It is referred to as the knowing-doing gap, a disconnect between knowledge in hand and associated action that advances that knowledge (Pfeffer & Sutton, 1999). As we learned in Chapters 1–3, many mid-career faculty (MCF) struggle with a lack of knowledge related to advancement criteria, policies, and practices. However, once that knowledge is obtained, MCF need to act on that knowledge to avoid the featured problem in this chapter—No formal strategy and poorly articulated advancement plans. This is a problem that plagues many during their mid-career years given the vagueness and length of this career stage.

I believe strongly that there should be no surprises when it comes to individuals' current and future standing in an organizational setting. Open communication with supervisors, collaborative performance reviews, and regular feedback solicited by the individual are necessary and useful to advancing along one's career path. Those same principles apply in higher education despite the unique nature of performance review processes in the academy. What I appreciate about Brad's experience, despite his disappointment, was that he received honest feedback, which enables him to have an accurate assessment of his current performance and allows him to identify the changes needed to advance.

In this chapter, I discuss the need to redefine work and productivity in the academy, which is particularly salient for those entering and firmly engaged in the mid-career stage. While all faculty across institution types felt the strain caused by the pandemic, women and faculty of color, especially those with young children, experienced extreme personal and professional challenges (Baker, 2021). Simply put, they need support. Using Brad's experience, I walk you through a five-step process to support strategy development and execution. I ground that work in a Scenario Planning Strategy Framework.

Redefining Work in the Academy

The global COVID-19 pandemic has forced a re-evaluation of the ways in which work and productivity are defined and measured at the individual and organizational levels. Organizationally, we are seeing this happen more explicitly in industry; higher education is certainly poised to move forward similarly should they so choose. Look no further than the global company Siemens, which plans to continue supporting remote work for two to three days a week. The CEO of Siemens, Roland Busch, makes a statement in response to life after the pandemic:

These changes will also be associated with a different leadership style, one that focuses on outcomes rather than on time spent at the office. We trust our employees and empower them to shape their work themselves so that they can achieve the best possible results. With the new way of working, we're motivating our employees while improving the company's performance capabilities.

(Bariso, 2021, para 5)

This approach to leadership is one based on mutual trust and an appreciation for the benefits of giving employees autonomy over their careers and their time. In fact, research has revealed that productivity remained consistent and even increased in some settings during the pandemic (Dahik et al., 2020; Maurer, 2020). However, the same cannot be said across the board for MCF in the academy. In fact, certain populations of faculty experienced crushing blows during the pandemic in terms of productivity and career advancement, which require new institutional and individual approaches to finding a way forward.

In the following section, I focus on the individual perspective of productivity and the need to re-envision career advancement processes moving forward by highlighting women faculty, particularly academic mothers, and faculty of color. Their experiences and resulting career losses will not be countered with short-term fixes; it is time for a reckoning about where work happens, how it is defined, and what is considered a contribution across the academy.

Perception vs. Reality

When the pandemic first hit, I found myself thinking I would use this time to tackle some of those projects that were on my "academic wish list." Mind you, my two children's schooling switched to fully remote, and I still had teaching and scholarly responsibilities with a husband who worked outside the home. Perhaps it was denial or naiveté about how long the pandemic would last and what I was capable of completing in that type of environment. However, I think Ahmed (2020) said it best:

And so, while it may feel good in the moment, it is foolish to dive into a frenzy of activity or obsess about your scholarly productivity right now. That is denial and delusion. The emotionally and spiritually sane response is to prepare to be forever changed.

(para 3)

While I certainly benefited from no longer commuting two hours a day to and from work, which all but eliminated the frenzied start and end to our days as a family, I initially struggled to get my footing. I would say, however, that within three months of the pandemic, I realized the "normal" I knew in the academy was no longer, and perhaps might not ever be again. I thought about my own process for making sense of this and how I would cope and advance my career goals, which I felt confident and capable of pursuing. I have been very deliberate about aligning the areas in which I engage across teaching, scholarship, and practice around my intended contribution (see Chapter 1), which is to help people advance in their careers. This alignment serves as a litmus test for me about what to say "yes" to and how my efforts can be in service to the areas in which I am expected to engage rather than about competing time commitments resulting in a zero-sum game. Nevertheless, I also felt deeply for my faculty colleagues who are not as privileged as I, a White woman full professor. My academic women peers were struggling, particularly those who are mothers, as were my faculty of color peers. Real concerns about career advancement, goals of full professorship, and leadership aspirations were tabled.

Women Faculty and Academic Mothers

Look no further than recent news headlines and you will quickly get up to speed about how this pandemic has affected women academics, particularly those with small children (Flaherty, 2020; Henderson, 2020; Kramer, 2020; Shalaby et al., 2020; Scheiber, 2020). Such strain is challenging for women in careers that follow an up-or-out trajectory, of which defines the academy. High-stakes promotions are on the line and women and academic mothers are feeling the tension. "The loss of months or more of productivity to additional child care responsibilities, which fall more heavily on women, can reverberate throughout their careers" (Scheiber, 2020, para 4).

Researchers reveal that women academics are taking this pandemic "on the chin" (Flaherty, 2020, para 1) in terms of their scholarly productivity (Krukowski et al., 2021). For example, Squazzoni and colleagues (2020) found that during the onset of the pandemic women academics submitted proportionally fewer manuscripts compared to their male faculty colleagues; the deficit was most pronounced for early career cohorts of women academics. Their overall findings revealed this time also created potentially cumulative advantages for male academics, only increasing the gender disparities that exist in the academy. Compounding the challenges to scholarly productivity for academic women is the disproportionate service burdens that have surfaced because of the pandemic (Shalaby et al., 2020). "The ongoing health crisis further deepens these disparities with considerable long-term consequences for female faculty research productivity and career advancement" (Shalaby et al., 2020, para 2).

Recently, a colleague and I proposed a call to action to re-envision work models and faculty development in a post-COVID era (Baker & Lutz, 2021). We focused specifically on the issues women faculty and academic mothers face. Many institutions are pausing and extending tenure clocks, and while that is a short-term fix, that approach alone is insufficient. Women and faculty of color need support now as they wait for institutional policies and practices to catch up to their realities in the academy.

Faculty of Color

It is important to reiterate that the pandemic has not created the inequities present in the academy experienced by women and faculty of color; they have been present for decades (Huston, 2005). However, the pandemic highlights the juxtaposition of privilege and inequality, signaling the need for new models of faculty support: "A pandemic naturally highlights privileges, such as financial security and access to mental health care. It also amplifies the mental, physical, social, and economic impacts attributable to preexisting inequities in academia" (Malisch et al., 2020, para 1). As Dr. Katherine Rowe, President of the College of William & Mary noted, one positive outcome of the pandemic is making the invisible labor of women and faculty of color across the academy, visible (McMurtrie, 2020).

Misra and colleagues (2021) urged the academy to implement engaged interventions, given the academy is likely to become less diverse and inclusive because of the immense pressure and negative career consequences women and faculty of color are experiencing. In their article, they provide a greater context in which women and faculty of color are operating within and outside of the academy. For example, Black, Indigenous, and Latinx communities have been disproportionately impacted by the pandemic in the areas of unemployment and healthcare, which places greater strain on faculty members from these communities as they care for loved ones. "Women and faculty of color have also been on the front lines in supporting vulnerable students, with Black, Indigenous and Latina women particularly burdened with mentoring and service work" (Misra et al., 2021, para 5). Despite the critically important work of supporting students from marginalized communities as they manage the challenges exacerbated by the pandemic, that engagement does not count in tenure, promotion, and advancement considerations (Bohanon, 2020). Such engagement takes an emotional, as well as professional, toll on productivity and career advancement.

The academy is forever changed as a result of the pandemic. Invisible work is now visible; populations of faculty are disproportionally disadvantaged and are in need of institutional and individuals supports.

It is both time to redefine productivity in the academy and to provide tools and resources to faculty to help them assert agency over their own career progression during mid-career.

Returning to Brad's Experience

Brad, like so many of us, is doing the right things generally. He is being thoughtful about his goals, has a clear picture about where he is headed, and understands what he needs to accomplish to get there. However, he also became deflated after interactions he had with his department chair and trusted peer, which revealed a disconnect between perception and reality. The pandemic seemed to exacerbate this disconnect based on Brad's assessment. I think we have all been there and felt the disappointment of an assessment that does not match our own perceptions of our contribution and professional progress. Brad attended a professional association workshop I delivered just before the pandemic hit. He shared his story with me at the workshop, and we connected after to work through his concerns. Our work sessions continued well into the pandemic.

Returning to Brad's situation featured in the opening case, ask yourself the following questions: What stands out to you? Does Brad's situation sound familiar? If so, in what ways? What advice would you offer Brad to move past his disappointment and on the path to achieving his career goals, even if later than he hoped? Write down your thoughts and observations in the space provided.

_____

_____

_____

_____

_____

_____

_____

Relevant Facts

Brad is clear about his goals and has a grasp on what he needs to do, broadly speaking, in order to achieve those goals. We know he has two goals: Earn full professorship and deanship at his institution. Brad is aware that in order to become a dean, he must earn the rank of full professorship. Brad also has a timeline in mind for achieving these goals. Since the deanship is a rotational position on his campus, missing that window means waiting for another recruitment cycle to pass.

Brad received feedback about his progression that is counter to his proposed timeline. After taking a step back to reflect on the feedback, Brad realizes his peers are correct; Brad needs to recalibrate to ensure his next three to four years are advancing him in the ways he needs to both earn full professorship and to be competitive for the deanship. He also wants to be realistic about this plan given he is re-launching it during the pandemic.

Key Stakeholders

Brad's department chair and trusted colleague are two vitally important members of Brad's network of support. Brad has regular meetings with his department chair, a senior colleague in his department, and reaches out once or twice a semester to secure the department chair's feedback and thoughts on a variety of professionally focused topics. Brad shared that he considers his department chair to be a wonderful and beloved mentor who "has never steered him wrong." As a man of color, Brad knows and values the importance of this mentorship.

Brad's colleague on campus joined the university two years prior to Brad. They met at a professional development workshop and stayed connected ever since, despite being in different divisional areas at the institution. Similar to Brad's department chair, his colleague is someone for whom he has a great deal of respect and values his opinion and career instincts. They bounce ideas off each other regularly and confide about their successes and areas of opportunity. In Brad's words, "I trust these two implicitly and have a great deal of respect for them and what they have accomplished professionally."

Needed Information

When Brad first shared his story during the breakout session of the workshop, a few thoughts immediately came to my mind. I asked myself, why was the additional time needed? And, why three to four years? I was curious if there were certain timeframes or precedents in terms of time at the associate rank that are more common at Brad's institution that were at play.

Second, Brad did not initially communicate the issues that necessitated the additional time. It was unclear if the additional time accounted for his performance in certain expected areas or across all performance areas. Maybe his plan was simply perceived as going up too early, which would be viewed negatively by senior colleagues across campus and on the personnel committee. I knew more information was needed about the reasons behind the advice he received about adding additional years to his plan, specifically the substance of the feedback as important to re-evaluating Brad's timeline and associated action steps and plans.

Third, now that Brad received this feedback, I knew he was dejected. Note, he attended the workshop 6 months after having the second related conversation with his trusted colleagues, and it was obvious the feedback was still quite raw and painful for him. I was interested to learn more about his commitment to both goals and how the changed timeline would affect his motivation. In other words, was he still interested in the deanship if he had to wait another cycle? And, if not, what other professional aspirations did Brad have that would fill that void until he was eligible to self-nominate for the leadership position should he choose to do so in the future.

Finally, I knew it was important to have a visual accounting of Brad's plan and his accomplishments to date in relation to that plan in order to assess what was needed moving forward. Clearly, Brad was "behind" on this plan based on feedback from his department chair and colleague. We just needed to determine in what ways Brad fell short in order to develop a plan and execution strategy to ensure timely progress moving forward.

Case Summary

Two aspects of Brad's experience stand out to me. First, he was clear about his goals and aspirations. Further, he had some accompanying plans to go along with those goals. Second, he has a strong network of support at his institution and he feels comfortable asking for and securing feedback about his performance. These are two hurdles that many of our faculty colleagues struggle to overcome. For Brad, this provides a strong foundation from which to build and regroup. In sum, Brad needed to articulate a more explicit strategy to ensure timely progress toward his career goals, and to build in accountability measures that would support his overall efforts. I was confident this was achievable, even during a pandemic.

Tools, Strategies, and Resources

As we dive into the tools, resources, and strategies that can help Brad overcome his execution issues, let us first return to the notion of the knowing-doing gap introduced earlier in the chapter (Pfeffer & Sutton, 1999). While situated in the context of organizations and their failure to execute well laid out plans, it is a case of knowing too much and doing too little in return. The knowing-doing gap, according to Pfeffer and Sutton (1999), can be traced back to one fundamental issue—allowing talk to substitute for action. I think we all have worked for a boss or organizational leader who is quite adept at communicating key talking points that resonate with community members and securing buy-in. You walk out of meetings feeling energized by what you just heard because all the right "buzz words" were addressed. Yet, when you step away and evaluate what you just heard, you realize those plans are not truly grounded in a strategy that helps explain why these particular initiatives as aligned with an organizational vision and mission. Instead, it sounds more like a bunch of seemingly disparate initiatives with no unifying theme leaving you to wonder how success can be achieved. Having goals and developing plans is critical to success. Nevertheless, if those plans are not accompanied by explicit strategies to execute them effectively, organizations fall victim to the knowing-doing gap. Individuals do as well.

Situating the knowing-doing gap in the context of the MCF stage and the academy, we know that lack of clarity and information is a problem. Chapter 3 provided the "knowing," that is, the guidance on how to secure and use information as an organizational frame, while this chapter provides the "doing." In the following section, I walk you through steps to construct your strategy in order to execute your plans successfully in order to advance toward your intended career goals.

Executing Your Strategy

According to Cote (2020) "strategy execution is the implementation of a strategic plan in an effort to reach organizational goals" (para 2). Execution must account for organizational structures, systems, and operational goals in order to achieve success, or to at least position yourself for success. Cote (2020) outlines a five-step process for organizations to follow to support successful execution. I have adapted those steps to support individual strategy execution as necessary to supporting career advancement in the academy; the steps serve as a guide and one that Brad and I worked through together as we re-assessed and re-established his plans moving forward.

Step 1—Commit to a Strategic Plan. The first step toward successful execution is securing buy-in on your strategic plan. For MCF, this may mean talking with your department chair, dean of faculty, and/ or academic dean to ensure your plans have the potential to move you toward your goals. I also think this involves conversations with family members and loved ones whose support is needed, but who also are affected by your professional pursuits. Before you can commit to a strategic plan, you need to be clear about your vision, primary objective(s), and lay out a timeline for achieving your goals.

Step 2—Align Actions to Strategy. Cote (2020) notes the importance of aligning *jobs* to strategy, which is applicable in organizations. For MCF, I urge you to align your *actions* to your strategy. This step entails connecting your actions across the areas in which you are expected to be "excellent" (otherwise known as your promotion criteria or other metrics that are associated with your career advancement goals). Further, you must ensure those actions highlight your institutional value add. Mid-career is a challenging time and you cannot afford to engage in actions that compete for your time rather than working in complementary ways.

Step 3—Communicate Plan with Network Members. While Cote's Step 3 highlights how communicating clearly will empower employees, for MCF this step involves communicating purposefully and often with your network of mentors. Brad has excelled at this step, engaging his department chair as well as a trusted colleague on campus in his career advancement process. While it is not good to second-guess actions, Brad realized that if he shared his plans earlier in the process as he was creating them, he might have been able to avoid the situation he now faces. Writing down your goals and plans and displaying them in a place where you can reference them regularly might also encourage you to mention them during your regular conversations with your network. Do yourself a favor and read *Write it Down Make it Happen* by Henrietta Anne Klauser (2001). It is a quick read and helps you harness the power of putting pen to paper.

Step 4—Monitor Progress. You absolutely must engage in regular self-assessment and peer assessment that helps you monitor your progress. Brad's conversations with his department chair and colleague served as a good progress check for him. While disappointed by what he heard, Brad was also grateful he had these conversations at the time he did which he believes helped him avoid potentially more visible, disappointing career issues in the future. This step is all about identifying and implementing accountability measures that can include peer support, regularly scheduled meetings with a supervisor or others familiar with your work.

Create self-imposed timelines and deadlines, engage in friendly reviews, and schedule meetings with previous members of your institution's personnel committee to gather feedback and hold you accountable. You should have started identifying these accountability measures as you were working through your career progression framework in Chapter 3. Build on those ideas here as part of your strategy execution planning as you look ahead.

STEP 5—BALANCE INNOVATION AND CONTROL. As Cote (2020) notes, "To leverage innovation and maintain control over your current strategy implementation, develop a process to evaluate challenges, barriers, and opportunities that arise ... What pieces of the strategy are non-negotiable?" (para 24). I would argue that your goals are non-negotiable and you need to be clear about what is not on the table in terms of adjustments to your strategy. Perhaps family time is non-negotiable, which means you need to build this in to your execution strategy. If we have learned anything at all from the COVID-19 pandemic, anything can change at a moment's notice. It is important to be clear about priorities and the values grounding your career aspirations. Let those be the drivers guiding your strategy execution plans. Use the following space to write down some ideas for each of these steps as you think about how best to effectively execute your strategy.

_____

_____

_____

_____

_____

_____

_____

_____

_____

_____

_____

_____

_____

_____

_____

_____

_____

_____

_____

_____

_____

_____

_____

_____

_____

_____

_____

   While these steps are critical to ensuring success, they alone are insufficient to helping you execute plans effectively. I believe in the importance of grounding them in a strategy framework that helps structure
your thinking, analyzing career issues that may arise, and anticipating
scenarios as you advance along your career journey. In the next section,
I introduce you to the Scenario Planning Strategy Framework to facilitate
brainstorming possible future scenarios and thinking through how those
scenarios could affect achievement of your desired career goals.

Scenario Planning Strategy Framework

Also referred to as scenario analysis and scenario thinking, a scenario
planning strategy framework is a tool that helps the user visualize possible
future events that may affect them (Schoemaker, 1995). This knowledge
then allows the user to anticipate possible issues and develop contingency plans to combat the possible issues that may arise. As I said earlier
in this book, life and work happen. Events can derail our plans that, at
times, cause feelings of disengagement. Once in that space, motivation
can be a challenge. However, if you can think through possible issues that
may arise as part of strategy execution planning, your career progression
plan is less likely to be disrupted because you already anticipated possible issues and planned ahead. The goal is to help you be as proactive
and anticipatory as possible, rather than reactive to events and issues
that arise.

Critical Scenario Planning Considerations

Erdmann and colleagues (2015) noted that while scenario planning has
proven to be a highly effective tool, there are fundamental considerations
to keep on the forefront as you employ this strategy execution framework. First, fight the urge to make decisions based on information you
have in hand. Instead, review all considerations that have the potential to affect your plans. This may include pulled funding due to institutional financial constraints or the early retirement of a departmental
colleague causing a teaching schedule shake up. Second, while you need

to anticipate a diversity of contributing factors, evaluate and prioritize those factors. Some may not be worth the time and energy; prioritize the ones that would be the most harmful to your career advancement and plan accordingly. Third, do not assume the next two years will mirror the previous two years. Do not assume the future will look like the past. Instead, engage your network of mentors (Step 3 above) to contribute to the development of your contingency plans. Secure their buy-in and support. Fourth, while being prepared helps you feel more confident about your approach, be wary of becoming overly confident. Even the best-laid plans can be disturbed. Instead, assess the impact each scenario may have on the successful achievement of your goals and think through alternatives that can still help you achieve success. Finally, you must re-evaluate your plans and monitor your progress. Plans should evolve based on a variety of factors. Encourage your network of mentors and loved ones to offer their input throughout the process as you assess your progress along the way.

Now that you have these working ground rules for employing a scenario planning strategy framework, I will walk you through the actual framework with some examples of how to use it.

Scenario Planning Visual

I prefer to use a two-by-two visual that accounts for various scenarios and associated implications (see Figure 4.1 adapted from Creately, by A. Athuraliya, 2021). This approach aids in decision-making, supports your learning and thinking, and helps you evaluate your career progression.

Using Brad as an example, let us walk through the two career advancement scenarios, Dimension #1 and Dimension #2, which he now faces as he re-envisions his career advancement plans. Dimension #1 is focused on the timeline for achieving full professorship. While his original plan was to earn full professorship in two years, it is clear to him based on feedback that will not be the case. He was told three to four years is likely more accurate. Now, it is up to Brad to decide and plan for either a three- or four-year runway. Scenario A (Figure 4.1) is focused on Brad earning full professorship in three years. Part of that scenario planning requires him to think through all the events, resources, and plans that need to be in place in order to meet the three-year timeframe. I asked Brad, what conditions must be present to achieve the goal? What obstacles might impede progress?

Scenario B assumes a four-year runway toward full professorship. Brad and I talked through all the possible reasons, professional and personal, he would miss the three-year timeframe, the pandemic being one of the primary reasons. This prompted Brad to think through and

Dimension 1—Full Professor

	Scenario A Implications	Scenario B Implications
Dimension 2—Dean	Full in 3 Years	Full in 4 Years
	Scenario C Implications	Scenario D Implications
	Full for 3 Years	Full for 4 Years

Figure 4.1 Scenario Planning Visual.

articulate contingency plans, but also to shore up what needs to happen as outlined in Scenario A to meet his new three-year to full professorship target. Hint: It would involve regular progress meetings with his department chair, frequent high-quality touch points with collaborators and self-imposed deadlines to ensure timely progress on projects, and one divisional colleague each semester to observe Brad's teaching to offer feedback on his newly developed courses.

Dimension 2

Dimension #2 is about his goal of earning a deanship on campus as the next step on his leadership pathway. Because of the new timeline for achieving full, it is clear Brad will miss applying for the deanship when the position becomes open. If he pursues and earns a three-year timeframe for full professorship, Brad will have to wait three years after earning full professorship to apply. If he pursues the four-year timeframe, Brad will have a two-year wait. Politically, Brad and I agreed that it was likely better for him to be a full professor for three years prior to securing a deanship, which means the goal of full in three years aligns better with his deanship goals.

Scenario C assumes Brad earns full professorship in three years. Working under that assumption, Brad and I began to think through the leadership opportunities, formal and informal, he should pursue to help him be more competitive for the deanship and to garner more campus visibility to informally help his case. We literally listed out internal and external leadership development opportunities, associated costs (financial and time), and key stakeholder support needed. Scenario D assumes Brad needs a four-year runway to earn full, thus resulting in him serving as a full professor for two years prior to pursuing a deanship. This shortened the list of leadership opportunities he could pursue, so we narrowed the list down to two opportunities, both of which we felt would be beneficial to him.

This scenario planning surfaced a critical dilemma for Brad. Does he earn full professorship sooner in order to be better prepared for a deanship, or does he wait the additional time as he looks toward full. For Brad, he envisions himself as an academic leader and possible long-term administrator. Therefore, our scenario planning focused on how to set him up for success on this leadership path. That means, Brad will pursue full professorship in three years. Doing so will give Brad more professional space to take advantage of leadership and professional development opportunities that will enable him to be better prepared and more competitive for the deanship.

Strategy execution and scenario planning are rooted in the knowledge that anything can happen, positive or negative, at any given time. Hearing earlier than expected about an accepted manuscript or losing funding that was critical to your success are issues that arise in the academy with regularity. The goal is to be prepared for the career events that come your way, and if possible, prepare for them to minimize possible disruptions that may be caused as a result. Having a clear strategy and plans to execute that strategy help you manage the ebbs and flows of life in the professoriate.

Chapter Summary and Next Steps

Knowing what to do to advance toward your career goals and actually *acting* on that knowledge are quite different. To get to this point in their careers, MCF have followed a path characterized by professional milestones. Yet, training in the professoriate is rooted in disciplines and unless that discipline involves an understanding about strategy and execution, MCF have the potential to come up short as they strive to execute their plans, the featured problem in this chapter (**No formal strategy and poorly articulated advancement plans**).

As highlighted in Chapter 3, clarity about your career goals and articulating plans to achieve those career goals is fundamental to career advancement pursuits. Nevertheless, you must also be strategic in how you execute those plans in order to be successful. In this chapter, I walk you through a five-step process to help you execute your strategy. Throughout those five steps you commit to your strategy, align your actions in service to that strategy, and engage your network of mentors for guidance and support. It is also imperative to build in account-ability measures and to develop a plan and metrics to measure your progress.

No one could have predicted the pandemic or the impact that pandemic would have on life and career. However, the bigger lesson that resulted from the pandemic is an important one—anything can change in a moment's notice. It is important to consider all the opportunities and barriers that may arise in relation to your plans. Account for those possi-bilities, in priority order, so that you are as prepared as possible for what may come your way. You will have already anticipated the challenges and opportunities and planned ahead.

References

Ahmed, A. S. (March 26, 2020). Why you should ignore all that coronavirus-inspired productivity pressure. *The Chronicle of Higher Education*. www.chronicle.com/article/why-you-should-ignore-all-that-coronavirus-inspired-productivity-pressure/?cid2=gen_login_refresh&cid=gen_sign_in

Athuraliya, A. (2021). The top 7 tried and tested strategy frameworks for businesses. *Creately*. https://creately.com/blog/diagrams/top-strategy-frameworks-for-businesses/#:~:text=Strategy%20frameworks%20are%20tools%20that,their%20solutions%20to%20their%20clients

Baker, V. L. (2021). Women in higher education: Re-imagining leadership in the academy in times of crisis. *Journal of Faculty Development*, *35*(1), 57–62.

Baker, V. L., & Lutz, C. (2021). Faculty development post COVID-19: A cross-Atlantic conversation and call to action. *Journal of the Professoriate*, *12*(1), 55–79.

Bariso, J. (2021, January 26). This company's new 2-sentence remote work policy is the best I've ever heard: Siemens' new remote work policy is a master class in emotional intelligence. *Inc.* www.inc.com/justin-bariso/this-companys-new-2-sentence-remote-work-policy-is-best-ive-ever-heard.html

Bohanon, M. (September 15, 2020). Pandemic expected to cause additional barriers to tenure for marginalized academics. *Insight into Diversity*. www.insightintodiversity.com/pandemic-expected-to-cause-additional-barriers-to-tenure-for-marginalized-academics/

Cote, C. (2020, November 17). 5 Keys to successful strategy execution. *Harvard Business School Online*. https://online.hbs.edu/blog/post/strategy-execution

Dahik, A., Lovich, D., Kreafle, C., Bailey, A., Kilmann, J., Kennedy, D., Roongta, P., Schuler, F., Tomlin, L., & Wenstrup, J. (2020, August 11). What 12,000 employees have to say about the future of remote work. *BCG*. www.bcg.com/publications/2020/valuable-productivity-gains-covid-19

Erdmann, D., Sichel, B., & Yeung, L. (2015). Overcoming obstacles to effective scenario planning. *McKinsey Quarterly, 55.* www.mckinsey.com/business-functions/strategy-and-corporate-finance/our-insights/overcoming-obstacles-to-effective-scenario-planning

Flaherty, C. (October 20, 2020). Women are falling behind. *Inside HigherEd.* www.insidehighered.com/news/2020/10/20/large-scale-study-backs-other-research-showing-relative-declines-womens-research

Henderson, E. (2020, December 3). Stay-at-home orders are hindering US academic productivity of faculty with young children. *News Medical Life Sciences.* www.news-medical.net/news/20201203/Stay-at-home-orders-are-hindering-US-academic-productivity-of-faculty-with-young-children.aspx

Huston, T. A. (2005). Race and gender bias in higher education: Could faculty course evaluations impede further progress toward parity? *Seattle Journal for Social Justice, 4,* 591. www.uis.edu/aeo/wp-content/uploads/sites/10/2014/09/Race-and-Gender-Bias-in-Higher-Education-Could-Faculty-Course-Ev.pdf

Klauser, H. A. (2001). *Write it down make it happen: Knowing what you want and getting it.* Simon and Schuster.

Kramer, J. (2020, October 6). The virus moved female faculty to the brink. Will universities help? *The New York Times.* www.nytimes.com/2020/10/06/science/covid-universities-women.html

Krukowski, R. A., Jagsi, R., & Cardel, M. I. (2021, March 4). Academic productivity differences by gender and child age in science, technology, engineering, mathematics, and medicine faculty during the COVID-19 pandemic. *Journal of Women's Health, 30*(3), 341–347. www.liebertpub.com/doi/10.1089/jwh.2020.8710

Malisch, J. L., Harris, B. N., Sherrer, S. M., Lewis, K. A., Shepherd, S. L., McCarthy, P. C. Spott, J. L., Karam, E. P., Moustaid-Moussa, N., Calarco, J. M., Ramalingam, L., Talley, A. E., Cañas-Carrell, J. E., Ardon-Dryer, K., Weiser, D. A., Bernal, X. E., & Deitloff, J. (2020, July 7). Opinion: In the wake of COVID-19, academia needs new solutions to ensure gender equity. *Proceedings of the National Academy of Sciences, 117*(27), 15378–15381.

Maurer, R. (2020, September 16). Study finds productivity not deterred by shift to remote work. *SHRM.* www.shrm.org/hr-today/news/hr-news/pages/study-productivity-shift-remote-work-covid-coronavirus.aspx

McMurtrie, B. (2020, November 19). Teaching: Reckoning with faculty burnout. *The Chronicle of Higher Education.* www.chronicle.com/newsletter/teaching/2020-11-19

Misra, J., Clark, D., & Mickey, E. L. (2021, February 10). Keeping COVID-19 from sidelining equity. *Inside HigherEd.* www.insidehighered.com/views/2021/02/10/without-intentional-interventions-pandemic-will-make-higher-education-less-diverse

Pfeffer, J., & Sutton, R. I. (1999). The smart-talk trap. *Harvard Business Review, 77*(3), 135–136.

Scheiber, N. (2020, September 29). Pandemic imperials promotions for women in academia. *The New York Times.* www.nytimes.com/2020/09/29/business/economy/pandemic-women-tenure.html?referringSource=articleShare

Schoemaker, P. J. (1995). Scenario planning: A tool for strategic thinking. *Sloan Management Review*, 36(2), 25–50.

Shalaby, M., Allam, N., & Buttorff, G. (2020, December 18). Gender, COVID, and faculty service. *Inside HigherEd*. www.insidehighered.com/advice/2020/12/18/increasingly-disproportionate-service-burden-female-faculty-bear-will-have

Squazzoni, F., Bravo, G., Grimaldo, F., García-Costa, D., Farjam, M., & Mehmani, B. (2020, October 16). Only second-class tickets for women in the COVID-19 race. A study on manuscript submissions and reviews in 2329 Elsevier journals during the pandemic. *SSRN Electronic Journal*. http://dx.doi.org/10.2139/ssrn.3712813

Part 2

Departmental and Institutional Perspectives

Chapter 5

Becoming an Effective MCF Mentor as Department Chair

Natalie, a social scientist, is a first-time department chair in a liberal arts college working her way through the position's three-year rotation. Natalie earned P&T two years earlier. She spent one of those years on sabbatical conducting research with "beloved collaborators and friends." Her department chair predecessor continued in the role for an additional year upon Natalie's return from sabbatical, so she could "establish myself as a newly tenured member of the faculty" prior to assuming the department chair position. During that second year, she focused on initiating a new scholarly project that was conceived during her sabbatical year. Natalie felt fortunate that she had (and has) such a supportive and accommodating department chair and role model. Many of Natalie's campus colleagues lamented about having to assume the department chair role as soon as they returned from sabbatical, which was all but detrimental to pursuing projects that arose during the sabbatical timing. Despite the support and excellent role model Natalie had through her department chair, Natalie felt overwhelmed and somewhat lost when she started the role, something she shared with her spouse regularly. While she felt confident she could "juggle all the roles and expectations," she also felt blindsided by increased roles and expectations. Natalie felt like "new expectations arose daily." To make matters worse, there was no formal department chair training at her institution. The academic dean opted to not host a formal department chair training given there were "only three new chairs" the year Natalie stepped into the role. Instead, she was given the "department chair handbook" (a binder with some notes and deadlines) and told to follow up with questions. As Natalie shared, "I don't know what I don't know which makes it hard to ask the 'right' questions." Given she was not

DOI: 10.4324/9781003201311-8

alone, Natalie reached out to the two other colleagues across campus who were in the same situation. As a collective, they have assumed an "it's us against them" approach to serving in and succeeding as first-time department chairs.

Many mid-career faculty (MCF) members across the academy know Natalie's situation quite well. In fact, you may be Natalie currently or you recently survived being Natalie in your department as you were thrust into a role that is institutionally necessary but woefully under supported. Research has revealed that the department chair role is one of the predominant leadership entry points in the academy (Baker et al., 2019). Yet, the department chair position is also the penultimate in terms of leadership aspirations for many faculty given the lack of leadership and professional development training that accompanies this role (Baker et al., 2019; Flaherty, 2016). It is this issue that is the featured problem in this chapter—**Disconnect between role expectations and available training and development to achieve expectations** as department chair.

Very few academics, unless their disciplinary field is in leadership, management, or higher education administration, have participated in leadership development as part of their academic or professional journeys prior to this point in their careers. Doctoral programs prepare future faculty (or practitioners) to be scholars in their respective fields predominantly, while some offer programs geared toward teaching or teaching assistantship opportunities to ensure future faculty have training and/or experience as teachers. Nevertheless, there is no formal dedicated leadership or administrative training that I was able to find that accompanies the doctoral student experience. Further, there are limited programs or initiatives of which I am aware that begin such development for early-career colleagues across the academy or targeted specifically at MCF members themselves. Institutions would benefit from implementing a succession management process to ensure faculty are prepared to assume their roles and responsibilities as department chairs and beyond should they so choose (Baker & Manning, in press). While such efforts would be useful, they are nearly nonexistent.

In this chapter, I discuss research and practice that outlines challenges and opportunities associated with the department chair role. I also highlight research that examines the intersectionality of gender, race, and leadership, noting the importance of leadership diversity to contributing to departmental culture and climate. We then return to Natalie's experience to offer ways in which to better support newly appointed department chairs before diving into the new department chair triumvirate, leadership, management, and personnel development.

It Is Not just about Teaching and Scholarship Anymore

The department chair role is a common position found across higher education, domestic and abroad. While the department chair position has some similarities to other mid-level management positions outside of the academy, such as fostering an environment of trust and collaboration, there are many unique nuances that accompany this role that require tailored professional development and leadership training (Flaherty, 2016). Most critical to being successful in this role is bridging administrative and departmental needs and expectations while supporting faculty members' growth and development as academics (and also managing your own professional advancement and evolution in the process). Perhaps Gmelch and Burns (1993) said it best, "While this dynamic tension between administration and academics is critical in order to maintain higher education institutions, it does place the department chair in a difficult position to mediate the demands of administration and concerns of faculty" (p. 260). Nearly 30 years later, that tension still exists and is compounded due to the ever-evolving state of higher education. Changing student demographics, a rise in the reliance on contingent faculty, and re-envisioned faculty needs in a post-pandemic era create a unique environment in which to serve as department chair (Gappa & Trice, 2010, Ouellette, 2020); an environment that is not for the faint of heart.

Department chairs new triumvirate involves leadership responsibilities (e.g., culture creation and maintenance, vision and mission setting, ensuring equitable workloads); management responsibilities (e.g., managing a budget, completing yearly performance appraisals); and personnel development, including advancing along one's own professional journey (e.g., teaching, scholarship, service) while attending to the developmental needs of departmental colleagues (Normore & Brooks, 2014). In his article, *Your To-Do List as Chair*, Jenkins (2016b) highlighted the primary responsibilities of chairs in higher education. For example, Jenkins (2016b) noted that department chairs must advocate for faculty while also representing the administration. At times priorities and needs align between these stakeholders, other times they are at odds. In addition, department chairs must work to build consensus while providing a forum in which to air grievances. Most important, according to Jenkins (2016b) is setting a vision, "...no matter how independent-minded individual department members might be—the department as a whole tends to take its cue from the chair. A chair who is generally positive fosters optimism among faculty, whereas one who is negative generates pessimism" (para 19). The department chair role sets the tone for the department and has the potential to model behavior, good and bad (Jenkins, 2016a).

In the following section, I highlight department chairs' challenges and opportunities based on research and practice. These serve as a starting point for new and seasoned department chairs as they think about the ways in which they are expected to serve their departments, institutions, and themselves throughout their time in this role.

Challenges

As with any leadership or managerial position, the department chair role is not without its challenges (Gmelch, 1991; Weaver et al., 2019). Comparable to mid-level managers in industry, a department chair must attend to the needs of individual faculty members, account for departmental considerations (e.g., programming, curriculum, students), and work in service to institutional imperatives. Of critical import is the environment in which the department chair position is situated, particularly in higher education institutions in which a tenure system is present. That environment often comes with expectations for performance with limited authority to hold others accountable for failing to meet theirs. During one of my research interviews with a faculty member who was also a department chair (Pifer et al., 2015) she shared:

> It's a tough spot to be in. There are no incentives to inspire good behavior and no punishments to address poor behavior. Such an environment breeds mediocrity among some faculty colleagues and leads to burnout for those faculty members who contribute.
>
> (Pifer et al., 2015)

At its core, the department chair role is about interpersonal relationships including with superiors, departmental colleagues, students, and other staff. Navigating these different hierarchical levels require varied approaches and strategies for communication. Anicich and Hirsh (2017) highlighted this reality in their research:

> Middle managers have a complicated relationship with power because power is activated and experienced in the context of interpersonal relationships. When interacting with our superiors, we naturally adopt a more deferential low-power behavioral style. When interacting with subordinates, on the other hand, we adopt a more assertive high-power behavioral style. Failure to conform to these role-based expectations can lead to social conflicts and confusion, so people are very good at learning how to play the part that is expected of them.
>
> (para 4)

Navigating these shifts in communication approaches and strategies can be challenging for department chairs in the academy given the unique aspects of academic work. For example, it is possible that as department chair you can have authority over a more senior colleague either in terms of rank and/or years of service (Pifer et al., 2019). This requires constantly accounting for and reconciling power dynamics, interpersonal relationships, and sometimes divergent needs. As we have heard many times in our prior research, the department chair role can be a lonely, isolating place (Pifer et al., 2019).

Related to interpersonal issues and lack of authority is the transient nature of the department chair role (Gappa & Trice, 2010). These are typically rotational positions among departmental colleagues. Department chair terms are typically three years long, with an opportunity to "re-up" for a second three-year term. While it is preferred to have tenured members of the department serve in the role that is not always possible, placing untenured colleagues in an even more tenuous situation. The temporary nature of the position means faculty colleagues will once again return to the department as a peer. Such a reality may cause department chairs to avoid addressing poor behavior for fear of future retaliation when a new occupant assumes the position.

Opportunities

Despite the associated challenges, there are a great deal of opportunities that accompany the department chair role. This position is *the* leadership point of entry and can serve as a springboard to future leadership and administrative opportunities on one's respective campus and beyond (Baker et al., 2019). We have all (hopefully) worked for a person who brings out the best in others, operates under a model of mutual respect and transparency, and is willing to listen to others. We should all seek to model and expect these behaviors from our leaders.

The department chair plays a critical role in setting the tone in terms of behavior, communication, and expectations. Specifically, the department chair is a shepherd of departmental culture and can certainly be instrumental in fostering a culture of inclusiveness, collegiality, and respect (Pifer et al., 2019). When such leadership is lacking, it can wreak havoc on departmental colleagues and students. I agree with Bowman (2002) when he noted, "Academic department chairs function as leaders when they focus on key aspects of organizational culture: mission, vision, engagement, and adaptability" (p. 159). The person occupying this role has a tremendous opportunity to create a work environment in which others feel supported and empowered; one in which talents, professional needs, and contributions are acknowledged and appreciated.

The department chair also has an opportunity to pay it forward by creating or enhancing existing departmental knowledge management systems that enable subsequent department chairs to benefit from already developed knowledge, processes, and infrastructures. In brief, a knowledge management system enables a department (or institution) to gather and organize collective knowledge and wisdom, including past drafts of proposals, prior meeting minutes and agendas, and key dates and expected deliverables (Gurchiek, 2007). The departmental knowledge can be cataloged to allow subsequent department chairs to have access to critical information and to see documentation of prior efforts and associated paper trails. It also creates a system in which no one needs to reinvent the wheel, but rather, faculty benefit from lessons learned and best practices developed over time. Such systems also help to create continuity, which is particularly important in situations with rotational leadership roles and in remote work environments as a response to the COVID-19 pandemic (O'Connell, 2020).

Finally, if viewed as a growth opportunity as opposed to an obligation, the department chair role can be used as a vehicle to build critical leadership and managerial skills. Identifying those deemed as effective department chairs and reaching out to schedule a time to connect creates opportunities to learn from others through coaching and mentoring. Seeking regular feedback from departmental peers and those in faculty development roles supports professional growth. Use this as an opportunity to enhance areas of strength and identify growth opportunities, with corresponding goals, to build a diversified toolkit of skills and abilities to succeed in this role and future leadership and administrative positions.

Gender, Race, and Leadership

I would be remiss if I did not highlight the intersectionality of gender, race, and leadership, particularly in the department chair role. The challenges women and persons of color experience when serving as department chairs and other formal leaders is well documented in the academy (Mullen, 2009; Schell, 2019). Scholars have also highlighted interventions to support these populations of leaders (Drange & Barnes, 2019; List & Sorcinelli, 2018). Despite the challenges, there are numerous benefits, thus making the case for fostering more inclusive leadership pathways and departmental climates in the academy (Chun & Evans, 2015).

Researchers have found that department chairs focused on and actively fostering inclusion create a more productive, collegial environment for all faculty, particularly women and faculty of color (Mickey et al., 2020). Some simple strategies include hosting regular chair meetings, implementing departmental mentoring programs, actively working to ensure equitable distribution of service assignments, and hosting department mental research talks. Furthermore, greater diversity in the chairperson position has benefits at the departmental and individual levels. Research by Langan (2019), for example, found that women department chairs help reduce gender gaps in publications and tenure for early career colleagues. In addition, they shrink the gender pay gap. The investment realized when actively working to improve departmental culture and climate can be high; thus pointing to the need for greater supports and training available to department chairs to help them rise to the occasion.

In closing, the department chair position is critical in higher education. It serves as a bridge between the administration and departmental faculty. Despite the associated challenges, particularly for women and faculty of color, there is a great deal of potential for this role to serve as a lever of change in the academy. The department chair sets the tone for expectations and behaviors. The position can be a source of innovation and help foster and develop the next generation of faculty and institutional leaders. However, these benefits cannot be realized unless leaders across the academy begin to view the department chair role as a strategic leadership position and entry point to advanced leadership opportunities.

Returning to Natalie's Experience

As we return to Natalie's experience, I want you to think about all the factors at play that either set her up for success or create a steep learning curve that makes success in this role nearly illusive. It is essential to be thoughtful about how success is defined and measured in the department chair role. Natalie is fortunate to be supported by a previous department chair who set a strong standard for serving in the role. However, according to Natalie, she does not know what she does not know, resulting in an environment in which asking the right questions to support her own advancement and knowledge acquisition becomes hindered.

Natalie is a peer of mine and employed at a member institution from a consortium of which Albion College is a member. She also attended a previous Academic Leadership Institute workshop I, along with my colleagues, hosted. Natalie and I have spent many conversations listening and offering advice to each other as we navigate some of the perils of mid-career, particularly those associated with being women in formal leadership roles.

As you think about the information provided in the opening case, ask yourself what does Natalie need to be supported in her new role? What steps can she take to support her professional development? What knowledge is critical to her success? Write down your reactions to what is known based on the information provided in the case and have some questions prepared you would ask Natalie.

_____
_____
_____
_____
_____
_____
_____
_____
_____
_____
_____
_____
_____
_____
_____
_____
_____
_____
_____
_____
_____
_____

Relevant Facts

Natalie is newer to mid-career having recently been tenured and promoted two years prior to stepping in as department chair. This is her first time serving in a formal leadership role on her campus. Natalie made some solid progress during her sabbatical in terms of a scholarly project that she developed during her time away from campus that she plans to pursue once assuming her administrative work. Natalie returned from sabbatical and served as a tenured professor in her department for an additional year before stepping into the department chair role the following year, a commitment her department chair made with her prior to earning tenure.

Two other peers on campus assumed the department chair role at the same time as Natalie. Given the few individuals assuming the role that given year, the academic dean did not provide formal training. Instead, each person was given a department chair handbook and were told to ask questions as they arise.

Key Stakeholders

Natalie is fortunate to have a network of mentors and peers to support her leadership journey. First, Natalie has a supportive former department chair who served in the role immediately preceding Natalie. In Natalie's words, this department chair is an "advocate" and works from "a growth mindset." This department chair also served as an excellent role model for working effectively in this capacity. Natalie knows this colleague will continue to be a resource and mentor as she traverses this role.

Natalie is also joined by the other two department chair newcomers on her campus. They have agreed to create a peer-mentoring group of sorts to help collectively manage the rigors of this new leadership position. This agreement was in response to a lack of formal training or guidance from their academic dean. Lastly, while not explicitly mentioned, seasoned department chairs on campus have the potential to serve as mentors, but that is an area to be further explored.

Needed Information

We need to get an understanding of the areas in which Natalie is expected (or hoping) to engage in addition to her responsibilities as department chair. For example, Natalie's teaching load, and gaining clarity on how, if at all, the department chair role affects that teaching load is crucial information and must factor into her professional development plans.

Also, we need to learn more about the scholarly project that she developed during her sabbatical and pursued upon her return. What is the anticipated timeline, who are the collaborators (if any), and how can her engagement in this work continue to factor into her professional endeavors and schedule? This presents a chance to think about how to leverage collaboration and perhaps provide opportunities to undergraduate student researchers to advance the work under Natalie's direction.

Natalie also needs to gain clarity on the regular tasks and deadlines that accompany the department chair role on her campus. She needs to look at these tasks and build a plan to address them in a timely manner. Natalie could solicit engagement from departmental peers and seek guidance from key stakeholders on campus (including current and previous department chairs who are deemed effective and well-regarded), as well as administrators on campus who can support her knowledge development in these areas.

Last, but not least, we need to learn more about Natalie's leadership aspirations in general. Is she merely taking on the department chair role given it is her turn in the department? Or, does Natalie have aspirations beyond the department chair role that we need to plan for in order to then leverage professional development opportunities with those aspirations in mind. In brief, we need to know what Natalie is currently expected to manage along with her professional priorities to help her create a plan that allows her to gain critical skills and to foster a collegial departmental environment for her peers.

Case Summary

Generally speaking, Natalie is better positioned to be successful as a new department chair compared to others who step into this role immediately following earning promotion and tenure. She has a strong department chair role model and advocate and other trusted peers in a similar position who can provide moral and professional support. Yet, despite those advantages, there is still a steep hill to climb given the lack of formal institutional training and assistance. In the next section, I offer a deeper look into the critical areas department chairs must engage and offer guidance to enable you to assert agency over your own development.

Tools, Strategies, and Resources

We return to the department chair triumvirate that was introduced earlier in this chapter to guide our discussion of tools, strategies, and resources to support Natalie and other newly appointed and seasoned department chairs: Leadership skills, management skills, and personnel development. As one assumes this role, the associated expectations and span of management or control (e.g., number of individuals for which a manager has direct responsibility) expand, thus requiring a broadening of skills and professional competence (Acharya et al., 2017). Unfortunately, the academy generally is not known for investing in department chair training to a level that ensures this role serves as a springboard to future leadership aspirations (Baker et al., 2019).

While Natalie is a thoughtful person, seeking to develop the needed skills and competencies to be successful in this role, not everyone in the academy is like her. We have all been led by the disengaged and frankly, checked out, department chair who is our "leader" in title only. Infrequent or nonexistent communication, no clear direction or vision, and little effort to bring departmental colleagues together can greatly undermine departmental culture and set the wrong tone for how to engage at the institution moving forward. Moreover, to believe this reality is only known or experienced by departmental colleagues is misinformed. A dysfunctional department reverberates across campus, affecting students, departmental faculty, and peers across campus.

In the following section, I introduce you to some of the critical knowledge considerations you must take into account. No matter how successful you are as a leader or manager, you will struggle to be effective if you lack the foundational knowledge needed to advance your departmental initiatives or to support the career advancement of your colleagues.

Knowledge Acquisition and Strategies to Acquire It

As with any mid-level management position, there is certain foundational knowledge you need to have in hand in order to perform your job, and associated role expectations, effectively. This can include, but is not limited to, key reporting deadlines; associated forms to complete those reports; dates and times of any regularly scheduled chair/director-level meetings; primary points of contact across campus such as committee chairs; fellow department chairs; administrative professionals in key offices; budgetary understanding; and standard events for which the department chair is expected to attend as departmental representative. Ideally, this information is captured in an institutional knowledge management system or minimally, a department chair binder, but that is not always the case. Capturing this knowledge and codifying it should become a priority for you to both support your own advancement in this position, and to ensure the next incumbent is prepared to be successful. Digitizing this knowledge is preferred to facilitate easier access; a lesson we all learned during the pandemic.

I am a big fan of learning from others and engaging in capacity building in the process. Every campus has key administrative professionals who have a wealth of knowledge in their heads. You need to schedule meetings with those individuals to access and absorb as much of that knowledge as possible. For example, at Albion College we had an administrative assistant to the provost who had been at the college for decades. She was the keeper of everything. She knew handbook language; she knew all the current (and most recent) committee chairs; she knew processes and how they evolved over the years. She had access to all institutional forms and managed to seamlessly do her job. Every campus has this person. Schedule meetings with them, ask questions, and learn from them. Ask for copies of all departmental chair forms that you are responsible for completing and the associated dates. Ask for advice on what makes an effective department chair. Ask about some of the most common mistakes department chairs make and how to avoid them. Ask what is "mission critical" for you to be successful starting out or returning to the department chair post.

Additionally, I strongly encourage you to meet with others across campus. Find out the institutional committees for which department chairs most frequently interact and the expected deliverables. Schedule meetings with those committee chairs to get a handle on related needs for the academic year. Reach out to the department chairs deemed most effective in the role. Schedule time to learn from them and ask how they manage those expectations while also advancing their own professional pursuits. Much like how it takes a village to support an undergraduate student through their collegiate experience, that same village is needed to ensure department chairs are successful, particularly those new to the role. Leverage your human resources and mentor networks to set yourself up for success. You need to assume agency over your growth process in this role.

Skill Development

A next step after gathering the necessary foundational knowledge is investing in your skill development. That skill development entails three areas: leadership, management, and personnel. Each of these areas are distinct yet complementary and require an investment of time and resources in order to fully cultivate. As Kotter (2001) so adeptly noted, "...leadership and management are two distinctive and complementary systems of action. Each has its own function and characteristic activities. Both are necessary for success in an increasingly complex and volatile [business] environment" (p. 3).

Now more than ever, we need individuals in the academy who are effective leaders *and* managers; able to envision a path forward, while ensuring their institutional peers are put in a position to succeed. This investment in professional development needs to start at the department chair level (and likely even before). Sans explicit programming delivered and assessed at the institutional level, you must invest in your own development as a department chair. In the following sections, I highlight some relevant tasks and responsibilities that span the department chair role, offering guiding questions and frameworks to consider.

Leadership Development

In Kotter's (2001) influential article, *What Leaders Really Do*, he highlights the differences between leadership and management, which serve as the foundation for the information shared in this section. Kotter emphasized the importance of leaders setting a direction, coping with change, aligning people, and motivating and inspiring others. These skills are salient for department chairs, particularly in light of the COVID-19 pandemic evolving higher education environment.

For example, consider working with departmental colleagues on articulating a departmental mission and vision. At the beginning of each academic year, revisit the mission and vision and talk through ways in which departmental colleagues are living those espoused values, where are shortcomings. Decide, as a collective, how you will each contribute in meaningful ways and how you will hold each other accountable. At the end of each academic year, determine what needs to be improved upon moving forward. The department chair needs to *lead* these efforts and serve as a role model for how to engage.

I think it is important to realize that your leadership extends beyond your departmental colleagues to include your students and alumni. They too need to see a strong leader to feel safe, supported, and "in good hands." Such efforts are particularly important in a post-pandemic era, as all of us in the academy work to cope with the changes we are all experiencing. One of the wonderful opportunities you have as department chair is to re-write the script. What kind of department do you want to work in; do you want your students to be members? What has been hindering the achievement of this ideal, and how can you contribute in a meaningful way to overcome those barriers? What support do you need to be the type of leader that advances these ideals? Note—Natalie posed these very questions via email to her departmental colleagues as a first action item after assuming the department chair position. As a group, they talked through them together at a departmental retreat before kicking off the academic year.

To help guide your efforts as you work through these questions and others, consider the use of a framework. I offer the Framework for Considering Equity, Diversity, and Inclusion in Academic Departments, which was introduced by Smith (2009) and further developed by Drange and Barnes (2019). The framework accounts for four main components, including: Faculty and student access and success; learning curriculum and research/scholarship; departmental climate and intergroup relations; and department viability and vitality. At the core is the departmental mission. Identify and codify what is critical, or non-negotiable, for you and your departmental colleagues across these areas. Once you make these determinations, you must manage the process for moving forward which I discuss next.

Management Development

Once you have an agreed upon vision, mission, and expected behaviors, you need to sharpen your managerial acumen by engaging in and delegating the day-to-day work that needs to be done to advance your departmental vision and mission. Kotter (2001) highlighted critical management tasks, which include coping with complexity. You achieve this aim by establishing plans as well as setting targets, allocating resources, and creating an assessment plan. You, along with departmental colleagues and other relevant stakeholders, need to be involved in this process at the planning *and* execution stages.

For department chairs, a mission critical topic includes allocation of resources to ensure equitable faculty workloads and rewards (O'Meara et al., 2021). A recent report that came out of The Faculty Workload and Rewards Project a National Science Foundation ADVANCE funded, collaborative, action research project, which engaged with 51 academic departments to promote equity in how faculty work is pursued, delegated, and recognized (https://facultyworkloadandrewardsproject.umd.edu/). A summary of that report found the following:

> Faculty from historically minoritized groups are disproportionately called upon to do diversity work and mentoring, while women faculty do more teaching and service. These activities are vital to the functioning of the university, yet are often invisible and unrewarded, leading to lower productivity and decreased retention.
>
> (p. iv)

Returning to resources offered through Columbia University's Office for Faculty Development and Diversity at Columbia, they present the notion of uniformity, which they define as equity and fairness (Drange & Barnes, 2019). To support this ideal, they offer a table titled Faculty Members Commitments Tracker. On this table, each departmental faculty member, main campus committees, and other key roles (e.g., mentor to junior faculty) are represented. The idea is to simply track, via check box, who is engaged in what activities to ensure departmental representation as well as equitable distribution of work responsibilities. While created to track committee engagement, a diversity of tables can be created that, for example, track engagement across key areas relevant to faculty workload (such as teaching, advising, scholarly engagement). These tables both serve to ensure equitable distribution of workload but to also highlight the great work your departmental colleagues are doing.

Personnel Development

In addition to leading and managing departmental needs, department chairs are tasked with supporting the career advancement of their colleagues. Unfortunately, most experiences we have with engaging in this task are informed by personal experience rather than formal training. Again, while not all practices from industry are relevant or useful in higher education, one industry practice that has a great deal of utility in higher education is the use of developmental career advancement appraisals. The goal—treat faculty as individuals, taking the lead on their own growth and development through collaborative goal setting. Once goals are identified, it becomes important to work with that faculty member to identify opportunities to achieve the outlined goals.

Formal occasions for goal setting and personal growth greatly diminish as faculty advance along their careers (Baker & Manning, 2021). As noted in Chapter 1, I have seen a diversity of approaches to yearly performance appraisals that range from very collaborative between the department chair and MCF member to very hands off, placing full responsibility for the appraisal in the MCF member's hands with little to no guidance. I encourage all new and seasoned department chairs to prioritize, at minimum, yearly career advancement conversations, focused on professional development and growth, which is critically important at mid-career (Baker & Manning, 2021). To support this process, I recommend completing the following six steps (adapted from Pulakos, 2009):

1   Review career advancement across the areas in which faculty are expected to engage (e.g., scholarship/creative activity, teaching, service)
2   Identify and write out goals for improvement and/or continued development across these areas
3   List explicit actionable steps to achieve goals
4   Define success; identify measures/metrics that align (including interim milestones)
5   Note resources in hand/resources needed to achieve outlined goals
6   Review, finalize, and schedule regular check-ins to assess progress (e.g., monthly, twice a semester, etc.)

Having this knowledge about your departmental colleagues allows you to be a better campus advocate on their behalf, and help them identify relevant professional development and training programs that support their growth. As a management professor, I talk regularly with my students about getting to know their employees, understanding their learning styles, identifying what motivates them, and trying to understand their personal and professional needs. Such an approach to engaging in a team creates a climate of trust, open communication, loyalty, and accountability. I cannot think of one faculty member with whom I have interacted who would not appreciate working in a department that could be described in this way. The department chair can, and does, set the tone for the work environment.

Chapter Summary and Next Steps

The department chair role is one of the most visible positions in higher education, serving as the bridge between the faculty and administration.

A well-prepared department chair sets the tone for the department and works as an advocate and sounding board for colleagues as they advance along their professional journeys. Yet, formal training and development is lacking. In fact, the paucity of department chair training across the academy has been described as "woefully inadequate" (Flaherty, 2016, para 1). It is this reality that grounds the featured problem in this chapter: **Disconnect between role expectations and available training and development to achieve expectations** for department chairs.

Serving as department chair is not simply business as usual or a mere extension of the academic work you engaged in prior to stepping into the role. Department chairs must manage a new triumvirate that spans leadership, management, and personnel development. In order to be successful, new (and seasoned) department chairs must actively work to increase their knowledge development *and* skill development. This chapter aimed to provide tools, resources, and strategies across the areas of leadership, management, and personnel development to provide insights into the areas in which to invest in your own professional growth. Despite the immense responsibility that accompanies this role, there are also a wealth of opportunities to set departmental direction and to foster a culture of collegiality, trust, and professionalism.

In the current chapter, the goal was to provide guidance on the needed knowledge and skills to work in service to your department, colleagues, and institution. Chapter 6 will continue this discussion, as I offer support to help you advance your own professional goals and journey; acknowledging the importance of needing and receiving mentorship to support your own evolution while serving as department chair.

References

Acharya, A., Lieber, R., Seem, L., & Welchman, T. (2017, December 21). How to identify the right 'spans of control' for your organization. *McKinsey & Company*. www.mckinsey.com/business-functions/organization/our-insights/how-to-identify-the-right-spans-of-control-for-your-organization

Anicich, E. M., & Hirsh, J. B. (2017). Why being a middle manager is so exhausting. *Harvard Business Review*, p. 2–5. https://hbr.org/2017/03/why-being-a-middle-manager-is-so-exhausting

Baker, V. L., Lunsford, L. G., & Pifer, M. J. (2019). Patching up the "leaking leadership pipeline": Fostering mid-career faculty succession management. *Research in Higher Education*, 60(6), 823–843.

Baker, V. L., & Manning, C. E. (2021). A mid-career faculty agenda: A review of four decades of research and practice. *Higher Education: Handbook of Theory and Research*, 36, 419.

Baker. V. L. & Manning, C. E. N. (in press). Preparing the next generation of institutional leaders: Strategic supports for mid-career faculty. *To Improve the Academy*.

Bowman Jr, R. F. (2002). The real work of department chair. *The Clearing House,* *75*(3), 158–162.

Chun, E., & Evans, A. (2015). *The department chair as transformative diversity leader: Building inclusive learning environments in higher education.* Stylus Publishing, LLC.

Drange, S., & Barnes, K. (2019). Improving department climate: Tools and resources for departments and department chairs. *Office of Faculty Development and Diversity in Arts and Sciences at Columbia University.* https://fas.columbia.edu/improving-department-climate-tools-and-resources-departments-and-department-chairs

Flaherty, C. (2016, December 1). Forgotten chairs. *Inside HigherEd.* www.insidehighered.com/news/2016/12/01/new-study-suggests-training-department-chairs-woefully-inadequate-most-institutions

Gappa, J. M., & Trice, A. G. (2010). Rethinking the chair's roles and responsibilities. *The Department Chair, 20*(4), 1–3.

Gmelch, W. H. (1991). Paying the price for academic leadership: Department chair tradeoffs. *The Educational Record, 72*(3), 45–48.

Gmelch, W. H., & Burns, J. S. (1993). The cost of academic leadership: Department chair stress. *Innovative Higher Education, 17*(4), 259–270.

Gurchiek, K. (2007, October 1). Few organizations have plans to stem brain drain. *SHRM.* www.shrm.org/hr-today/news/hr-news/pages/cms_023170.aspx

Jenkins, R. (2016a, April 25). *The top 5 faculty morale killers.* The Chronicle of Higher Education. www.chronicle.com/article/the-top-5-faculty-morale-killers/?cid2=gen_login_refresh&cid=gen_sign_in

Jenkins, R. (2016b, July 10). Your to-do list as chair. *The Chronicle of Higher Education.* www.chronicle.com/article/your-to-do-list-as-chair/

Kotter, J. P. (2001). What leaders really do. *Harvard Business Review.* https://hbr.org/2001/12/what-leaders-really-do

Langan, A. (2019). Female managers and gender disparities: The case of academic department chairs. *Unpublished Working Paper.* https://scholar.princeton.edu/sites/default/files/alangan/files/langan_jmp_current.pdf

List, K., & Sorcinelli, M. D. (2018). Increasing leadership capacity for senior women faculty through mutual mentoring. *The Journal of Faculty Development, 32*(1), 7–16.

Mickey, E. L., Kanelee, E. S., & Misra, J. (June 5, 2020). 10 small steps for department chairs to foster inclusion. *Inside Higher Ed.* www.insidehighered.com/advice/2020/06/05/advice-department-chairs-how-foster-inclusion-among-faculty-opinion

Mullen, C. A. (2009). Challenges and breakthroughs of female department chairs across disciplines in higher education. *Advancing Women in Leadership Journal.* Retrieved from www.advancingwomen.com/awl/Vol29_2009/Carol_mullen.pdf

Normore, A. H., & Brooks, J. S. (2014). The department chair: A conundrum of educational leadership versus educational management. In A. I. Lahera, K. Hamdan, & A. H. Normore (Eds.), *Pathways to excellence: developing and cultivating leaders for the classroom and beyond* (pp. 3–19). Emerald Group Publishing Limited.

O'Connell, B. (2020, September 25). Knowledge management in the age of remote work. *SHRM.* www.shrm.org/resourcesandtools/hr-topics/people-managers/pages/managing-knowledge-in-the-age-of-remote-work.aspx

O'Meara, K., Culpepper, D., Misra, D. & Jaeger, A. (2021). *Equity-minded faculty workloads. What we can and should do now.* ACE-ENGAGE Report.

Ouellette, C. M. (2020, October 27). A chair's life in 3 stages. *Inside HigherEd.* www.insidehighered.com/advice/2020/10/27/insights-new-department-chair-has-gained-during-pandemic-opinion

Pifer, M. J., Baker, V. L., & Lunsford, L. G. (2015). Academic departments as networks of informal learning: Faculty development at liberal arts colleges. *International Journal for Academic Development, 20*(2), 178–192.

Pifer, M. J., Baker, V. L., & Lunsford, L. G. (2019). Culture, colleagues, and leadership: The academic department as a location of faculty experiences in liberal arts colleges. *The Review of Higher Education, 42*(2), 537–564.Pulakos, E. D. (2009). *Performance management: A new approach for driving business results.* John Wiley & Sons.

Schell, E. E. (2019). Special Cluster on Gendered Service in Rhetoric and Writing Studies: III. Is it worth it to "lean in" and lead? On being a woman department chair in rhetoric and writing studies 1. *Special Cluster on Gendered Service in Rhetoric and Writing Studies, 21*(2), 308–333. https://cfshrc.org/wp-content/uploads/2019/05/Peitho-21.2-Spring-2019-FINAL-2.pdf#page=60

Smith, D. G. (2009. *Diversity's promise for higher education: Making it work.* Johns Hopkins University Press.

Weaver, L. D., Ely, K., Dickson, L., & DellAntonio, J. (2019). The changing role of the department chair in the shifting landscape of higher education. *International Journal of Higher Education, 8*(4), 175–188.

Chapter 6

Advancing Your Career Goals as a Department Chair through Mentorship

Adam recently agreed to serve as department chair for a second three-year term. He said he finally felt like he was hitting his stride in this role and characterized the first three-year term as "drinking from a fire hose" with a very steep learning curve. Fortunately, for Adam, he works in a department known across his community college campus as being collegial and welcoming. Adam is in the fine and applied arts department and is in his 15th year as an academic, having spent seven years at his current institution (he was a traveling spouse and was fortunate to find a position that he loves so much). While happy to continue as department chair, Adam is getting concerned about his own career advancement. His productivity greatly reduced the first three years in this administrative role, and he aspires to earn the equivalent of full professorship at his institution (at Adam's community college, he will earn continuing contract status). In Adam's words, "Taking on this administrative role and learning on the job while also managing a 3-4 teaching load did not leave much time for me to invest in my own professional development. I feel more confident in this role and have some great momentum with my courses. But, I am getting concerned about my advancement prospects and feel like I am starting from square one in terms of who I am as an artist." Adam is the most senior person in his department now, with few mentors in his disciplinary area at his institution. As he reflects on the past three years, he attributes his lack of productivity to his "unintentional disengagement from his professional association" and is eager to re-engage. Nevertheless, when he thinks about this need, he instantly gets overwhelmed and needs support to figure out those first few steps. As he shared, "I feel somewhat like a fraud given I am offering advice to my early career departmental colleagues

DOI: 10.4324/9781003201311-9

about how to advance, yet here I am struggling to make the first step to help myself."

Perhaps Gmelch (2002) summed it up best, "If it takes seven to fourteen years to achieve expertise in our academic disciplines, why do we assume we can 'build a chair' in a weekend seminar" (pp. 2–3)? This question posed nearly 20 years ago still characterizes the predominant approach to leadership development across the academy for department chairs and other advanced leadership positions (Flaherty, 2016), the focus of Chapter 5. In addition to a lack of formal training and development to support your performance in the position, there is also **limited access to mentors to support your career advancement while serving as department chair**, which is the featured problem in this chapter. Becoming a department chair does not mean one gives up their own professional goals and pursuits; however, research shows taking on this role can halt or hinder one's advancement to full professorship or the achievement of other career goals (Gmelch, 1991, 2015; Ouellette, 2020).

Despite the increased responsibility that accompanies assuming the department chair role, it is still possible to pursue your own professional and personal goals and pursuits with the right tools. Mentorship at this stage is critical and figuring out what type of mentoring you need is paramount to your success. Mentoring at mid-career is different; it requires varied strategies and approaches to ensure you surround yourself with trusted individuals who can help you advance along the various areas in which you are expected to perform and as aligned with your own goals. As noted by Dickens and Gademer (2018), mentoring in middle career is equally as important as it is during early career given it helps support technical and relational skill development along with providing career guidance while helping you make professional connections.

The aim of this chapter is to make a case for the importance of mentoring at mid-career while also equipping you with the needed knowledge and resources to foster your mentoring network. To that end, I feature research and practice by leading mentoring scholars to ground the tools and strategies offered throughout this chapter. First, I discuss why leaders need mentors too.

Why Leaders Need Mentoring Too?

"You just don't wake up with agency, you practice it," said Dr. Joy Gaston Gayles, Professor of Higher Education and Senior Advisor for Advancing Diversity, Equity, and Inclusion at North Carolina State University. Joy was a panelist for the "Mid-Career Faculty Pre-Conference Workshop" delivered at the American Educational Research Association (AERA) and she was offering advice to a group of mid-career session attendees about how to take ownership over their own professional journey and pursuits. What I appreciate about this comment is the focus on assuming agency as a learned or developed skill. One, that with appropriate guidance and practice, can be improved upon and work in service to advancing your goals. I serve as the workshop chair and work alongside others enthusiastic about building a mid-career faculty (MCF) community. Not surprising, workshop attendees were eager to learn tips and strategies to help them navigate their mid-career journey, many of them were in or soon to assume department chair and directorship duties. They found themselves a bit overwhelmed and in need of advice on how to manage all the moving parts and pieces. I am in the privileged position of both supporting others along their career advancement paths while also benefitting immensely from my engagement with scholars from across the country and globe as we learn and grow together. Joy's comment resonated so deeply with me and was a good reminder about the need to be deliberate in our own evolution, seeking to hone our skills by practicing them regularly.

A few years ago, I came across a great article in Forbes titled, *3 Reasons All Great Leaders Have Mentors (and Mentees)*, written by Brian Rashid (2017). The opening line caught my attention immediately: "Trying to do great things is difficult. Trying to do them alone is, more often than not, impossible. That is why all great leaders have mentors, and also mentor others" (para 1). He further elaborated by saying success is a team support, which highlights the importance of surrounding oneself with a group of mentors or advisors who provide a diversity of support and who play a diversity of roles in your life. We all need to surround ourselves with individuals who push us in different ways. For example, Rashid highlighted three key mentoring roles, the challenger (e.g., asks why, pushes you outside your comfort zone), the cheerleader (e.g., boosts self-esteem and confidence), and the coach (e.g., the wise veteran who imparts needed knowledge). I am fortunate to have several mentors for whom I am profoundly grateful, and those relationships have evolved over time, with some having moved into friendship while others are still firmly in the mentoring space. I can identify many individuals who fall under each of these categories, but what they all have in common—they tell me the truth, even if that truth is hard to hear.

In Chapter 5, I highlighted the knowledge and acumen needed to be successful as you build your skills across the department chair triumvirate of leadership, management, and personnel development. In this chapter , I focus on mentoring, specifically advice to help you build your mentoring network to advance your professional and personal goals and aspirations. In the following section, I discuss mentoring literature to help clarify what mentoring is, and is not, as well as highlight critical elements for mentoring at mid-career.

What Mentoring Is (and Is Not)

One of my mentors and dear friends Dr. Laura Gail Lunsford is an award-winning mentoring scholar and practitioner. She has published extensively in the field of mentoring and engages in the practice of mentoring both as a mentor and in service to organizations seeking to create a culture of mentoring. A great deal of her work focuses on understanding what mentoring is and is not (Lunsford, 2020; Lunsford, 2016), noting the differences of what mentoring looks like and what a person's needs are at different career stages.

As Lunsford so aptly notes, by the time a faculty member reaches mid-career, there is a "sink-or-swim mentoring philosophy which needs to be solidly stamped out and on and replaced with greater intention and attention" (Lunsford, 2020, p. 139). MCF research clearly illustrates the needs, challenges, opportunities, and required competencies to be successful are different at this professional stage as compared to those associated with early or late career stages of the professoriate (Baker & Manning, 2021). As a result, the mentors who supported you early in your career may not be equipped to be as effective for you at mid-career (Goldsmith, 2010; Lunsford, 2020).

Mentoring at mid-career still involves psychosocial and instrumental, referred to as career, support (Johnson & Ridley, 2018; Johnson & Smith, 2016; Lunsford, 2020). Psychosocial support involves listening and building confidence while supporting you unconditionally. Important, however, is providing feedback (Lunsford, 2020). It is impossible to advance along your career if you are unwilling to receive honest feedback and you do not foster relationships in which honest feedback can be delivered. Career support includes advocacy and providing access to one's social capital; pushing someone beyond their boundaries while providing pathways and resources to be successful in that pursuit.

In addition to psychosocial and career support, Lunsford also highlights the importance of personal growth support, sometimes referred to as holistic mentoring, at mid-career (Johnson & Smith, 2016; Lunsford, 2020). Personal growth includes "helping you to realize your career vision and respect your work-life balance which may well be shaped by your family and personal priorities" (p. 15). Lunsford further explains, "Most importantly, expect your mentor to affirm both your professional identity and your sense of self..." (Lunsford, 2020, p. 150). The inclusion of personal growth as an aspect of mentoring is vital at mid-career given what research and practice tell us about how the faculty experience and expectations evolve, despite the ways in which personal and professional responsibilities intersect. Personal growth mentoring and related guidance helps the MCF member begin to think through the "I have tenure, now what?" question.

Critical Elements of Mentoring at Mid-Career

One of the breakout sessions in the AERA MCF workshop addressed mentoring at mid-career. Dr. Rich Reddick facilitated the topic and subsequent conversation. Reddick serves as the associate dean for equity, community engagement, and outreach at the College of Education and is a professor in educational administration at The University of Texas at Austin. Reddick is also a dear friend, colleague, and mentoring expert in the field. As part of the breakout session, Reddick shared his experiences with mentoring in the academy and talked about the importance of fostering a mentoring network to navigate mid-career. He highlighted four primary areas in which mid-career mentoring should take into account: scholarship, life circumstance (e.g., family, lifestyle, interests outside of work), professional aspirations (e.g., leadership, promotion, public scholarship), and campus/community service (e.g., working on issues you care about, issues that are meaningful and visible) (Reddick, 2019, 2020). These are the areas in which MCF must engage and manage to traverse this stage of their careers successfully.

While working in smaller groups, Reddick offered guidance that spans the areas including support from leadership, seeking mentorship, managing mentors, peer mentors, mid-career mentoring hazards, and looking ahead. In terms of support from leadership, Reddick noted the importance of engaging your department chair and dean, informing them of your career goals and aspirations. Reddick talked about the level of visibility tenured faculty members have; he urged attendees to leverage that visibility through thoughtful engagement with the larger college or university. He also shared the importance of seeking leadership opportunities on campus, through professional organizations, and through professional development.

When seeking and managing mentors, Reddick urged mid-career attendees to foster mentorships locally and nationally/internationally. This advice aligns with research that found early career faculty members rely on and are in need of mentors at their institutions, while MCF need mentors from outside their institutions (Law et al., 2014; Lunsford et al., 2017). As Reddick (2019, 2020) shared, "Think of promotion as a national discussion on your career—it's important to have perspectives and feedback on your body of work" (Reddick, 2019, 2020, Mid-Career Mentoring, Handout). This feedback aligns with his advice on managing your mentors, namely resist the urge only to have one mentor and never underestimate the power and importance of mentoring at a distance, especially as higher education and MCF roles and responsibilities become more digital.

While peer mentoring can and does play a role at all career stages (Baker et al., 2020; Willingham-McLain et al., 2019), it is critically important for MCF, particularly for women and faculty of color in leadership positions (Curran et al., 2019; List & Sorcinelli, 2018). Reddick urged attendees to think about how peers and near-peers could support research, professional, and lifestyle goals. The shared career (and possibly life) stage allows for mutual understanding and lived experiences.

Reddick concluded his breakout session by highlighting mid-career mentoring hazards such as toxic relationships and the ways in which mentoring relationships evolve (and dissolve which is ok). Perhaps most powerful, tying back to Joy's comment earlier, is the agency you have over the mentorship you need, want, and knowing when it is time to move on from the mentorship that is no longer a value add. As Reddick simply stated, "Remember, it's your career." This is a reminder that we can all benefit from mentoring as we advance along our own mid-career and leadership journeys.

As you might have guessed by now, I am fortunate to be surrounded by an amazing group of individuals who study, engage in, and consult in the areas of mentoring. Their thoughtfulness and experience have been a benefit to me and the many others for whom they support. A big takeaway from this section and chapter—mentoring matters, especially at mid-career. Nevertheless, the mentoring strategy you employed up to this point in your career likely needs re-vamping as you seek to manage your department chair role and career advancement.

Returning to Adam's Experience

As we return to Adam's experience, I was struck by something profound as I drafted this chapter—the lack of resources or research dedicated to the mentoring or training and development of department chairs, whether newly appointed or a seasoned veteran. This reality was highlighted by Gmelch (2015) and is still an issue presently despite the recognition across the academy for the importance of investing in institutional leaders along the leadership pipeline. A significant amount of literature discusses the primary tasks department chairs engage in (Jackson, 2019), yet few studies examine the mentoring needs of department chairs across institution types as aligned with their primary responsibilities. Even fewer resources exist that explicitly highlight the importance of or provide guidance to support department chairs in their own career advancement while juggling the myriad roles and responsibilities bestowed upon them. Adam is a near-casualty of this reality.

As you read Adam's story in the opening case, what information stands out to you? Perhaps you are Adam struggling to get your footing, fearing you will be stalled in your career for the foreseeable future (or perhaps permanently). Alternatively, maybe you fear you will become Adam if you fail to figure out how to manage to be a department chair while advancing in your own career. Ask yourself, what is most salient about Adam's situation and what support does he need? Write your thoughts down in the space provided, and we will tackle Adam's needs together.

Relevant Facts

Adam is a seasoned academic, both in terms of tenure in the academy and as a department chair. He is about to begin his second three-year term as department chair and is the most senior person in his department. Fortunately for Adam, he is a member of a highly regarded department on campus, one that is described as collegial. He is finally getting settled in the department chair role after experiencing a steep learning curve, and much to his surprise, Adam enjoys serving in this leadership role. As a faculty member in a community college, he has a significant teaching load (3–4) and academic advising load in addition to his administrative responsibilities.

Adam is concerned that his engagement in this role could hinder his professional goal of earning full professorship (e.g., continuing contract status). Despite his best intentions, Adam's creative activity tapered off while serving as department chair, and he fears that decline will continue.

Key Stakeholders

One of Adam's biggest areas of need is fostering and managing a mentoring network. Adam's lack of engagement in his professional association makes cultivating a mentoring network challenging. Additionally, Adam's experience illustrates the loneliness that accompanies the role of department chair. Garnering peer mentors proves difficult because he is the senior person in his department with few peers on his campus in other areas across his division of fine and applied arts.

However, Adam is at an advantage due to his high-functioning department. This reality eliminates some stress that department chairs face, mainly managing challenging personalities. Moreover, as Adam shared, his departmental culture makes for a pleasing work environment given "everyone gets along so well." Adam can leverage this collegiality as he seeks to delegate some departmental responsibilities.

Needed Info

There are several areas worth exploring in relation to Adam's experience and needed next steps. First, we know Adam has the goal of earning the equivalent of full professorship at his institution; we need to know the timeline he is aspiring to along with the institutional requirements and criteria to achieve that goal. Related, understanding what role, if any, administrative duties factor in is also necessary.

Second, we need to find out the areas and tasks in which Adam spends the majority of his time. Even the most productive and disciplined individuals have room to make schedule adjustments to ensure greater productivity (with fewer projects). Adam needs help re-examining his schedule, his daily/weekly activities, and time spent engaging in those tasks to understand how to be more efficient with his time. Related, engaging in activities that help to identify a prioritization of tasks would be useful. I think all of us can identify a task or project (or two) that is not advancing our personal or professional pursuits in any meaningful way. Those activities are prime suspects to be removed from our to-do lists permanently.

Third, we need to determine how removed Adam is from his disciplinary roots, specifically in terms of his engagement in his professional association and other related organizations. As we stated earlier, MCF need and rely more frequently on mentors from outside of their institutions at this stage of their careers. Professional conferences and associations provide prime opportunities to identify and engage with much-needed mentors. Understanding the barriers Adam must manage such as time, financial constraints, and lack of creative work are all factors that need to be addressed.

Finally, Adam needs help re-envisioning himself as an artist. Understanding Adam's values, passions, and interests will be critical to helping him think through what this next phase of his artistry looks like and what he wants it to represent. Helping him articulate these complementary points and figuring out what place they occupy in his professional plans is necessary.

Case Summary

Adam faces a crossroad like so many MCF members face—the need to re-envision and sometimes re-establish one's scholarly or creative identity. This process is even more challenged when engaging in administrative and leadership roles that require so much yet often provide so little dedicated supports to manage expectations. I was working with an MCF colleague, who connected me with her family friend, Adam. I found Adam to be deeply thoughtful, pleasant, and very much in need of guidance. I knew that if Adam had a few tools and resources at his disposal, he would be just fine. It is those tools and resources I describe in the next section.

Tools, Strategies, and Resources

If you do not have a copy of *On Being a Mentor: A Guide for Higher Education Faculty* by W. Brad Johnson, do yourself a favor and get a copy.

•

Brad is an internationally recognized mentoring scholar and practitioner and has been a great source of support to me over the years. His guide serves as an excellent resource for faculty and institutional leaders on how to engage as mentors, how to create a culture of mentoring, and how to appropriately assess and reward effective mentoring. His work, along with the work of Laura Lunsford, serves as the foundation of the tools and tips offered in this section. Specifically, I draw on their work in which they outline how to facilitate effective mentorships (Johnson, 2015; Lunsford, 2020). This knowledge can, and should, inform how you think about assessing your current mentoring network and fostering new relationships as it evolves. First, it is imperative to determine what mentoring support you need to help advance your professional and personal goals.

Mentoring Needs Inventory

The first step is knowing you need mentorship, and I hope the literature and insight offered in this chapter help you realize the importance of mentorship, particularly as you navigate leadership responsibilities while simultaneously managing your own career advancement. This phase of one's professional and personal journey requires a more nuanced approach to successfully traversing this stage. Given that Adam is the most senior person in his department and his most beloved mentor and colleague retired from the institution, Adam's mentoring network needed a refresh after undergoing a more strategic review.

A wealth of literature highlights the value of having a diversity of mentors, often referred to as a developmental network, particularly in the academy (Higgins & Kram, 2001; Sorcinelli & Yun, 2007). However, it is not simply a matter of having many mentors, but rather having the "right" mentors to help you develop in your areas of need. This fundamental principle reminds me of a famous exchange from the movie Miracle, in which Craig Patrick (assistant general manager and assistant coach) comments to Herb Brooks (head coach) about his proposed player line up with several days of hockey tryouts remaining. He says, "You're missing the best players." To which Herb Brooks responds, "I'm not looking for the best players, Craig, I'm looking for the 'right' ones" (O'Connor, 2004). The goal is to assemble a team of mentors who elevate your play and help advance your goals and aims.

You need to engage in a "mentoring needs inventory" or what Lunsford (2020) refers to as a "gap analysis." A mentoring needs inventory or gap analysis helps you evaluate the status of your current mentoring network to identify the areas in which you need to enhance your mentoring network (e.g., professional, professional, growth). It also provides an opportunity to prioritize those areas based on your overall professional goals. I will walk you through the five steps below.

1   List your current mentors including names, affiliations (e.g., institution, discipline professional association)
2   Describe the type of mentoring for each identified mentor (e.g., career, psychosocial, personal growth) and the support they provide
3   Return to your professional needs and goals, write them out
4   Indicate which mentors provide support in service to the professional needs and goals you just outlined
5   Ask yourself, are there professional goals and needs for which you are not receiving adequate mentorship (or perhaps none at all)? How often do I engage with the mentors identified? Has a significant amount of time passed since our last interaction? If so, why?

It is these identified "gaps" that provide direction on how to broaden your mentoring network (Lunsford, 2020).

This five-step exercise opened Adam's eyes. While he was aware his mentoring network was sparse, it was not until he saw it in writing that he realized how neglectful he had been in terms of seeking mentorship to support his advancement in the field and engagement in the role of department chair. As we talked, he realized he had not sought mentorship on any aspect of his professional pursuits in the past two years. After some reflection, Adam surmised that he felt embarrassed about that reality, and his productivity confirmed that. Further, he was not sure what support he needed to overcome this lull; therefore, he focused on other areas in which he could "move the needle" and for which there were immediate deadlines with local implications (e.g., completing year-end reports and annual evaluations for departmental colleagues).

I encourage you to be aspirational as you think about your professional goals and needs. Perhaps you aspire to secure more external funding or to increase your visibility beyond your institution. Whatever the goal and need, be deliberate in identifying mentors who can help you achieve those aspirations. Using the space provided, work through these steps.

_____

For Adam, writing these ideas down helped initiate a spark, allowing him to have a first step to take to re-establish his identity as an artist. According to Adam, one of his biggest hurdles was knowing where to start and mapping out his mentoring inventory helped alleviate some of that apprehension. Writing out his professional, personal, and growth needs allowed us to collaboratively think through the type of mentors to help Adam meet those needs. We also talked about colleagues for whom he admired and why he admired them. We added these individuals to the list of possible future mentors. We then brainstormed strategies for reaching out to these individuals to set up a first meeting with the goal of debriefing after those sessions about who might be a good fit for Adam. I really emphasized that these first meetings were just that, an opportunity to get to know these individuals a bit more and learn about their experiences to date. Rather than walking away from the meetings with a confirmed mentor, the goal was to obtain knowledge about the person that would inform the next steps should Adam choose to move ahead.

Building Your Team of Supporters—But First...

In keeping with the team metaphor, I think it is essential to build a winning team of supporters that will help you grow professionally and personally. Building your team requires deliberateness and a frank assessment about what you do, and do not, bring to the table as a prospective mentee. Be clear about what your "deal breakers" are. At this stage in your career and life, you need to assume agency over the process. Assuming that agency is a necessary part of preparing your mentoring needs inventory, for example. Moreover, frankly, it is necessary to look at your current mentors to decide if they are still meeting your needs. If they are not, those mentorships may need to transition.

Before reaching out to foster new mentorships (and perhaps re-envisioning existing ones), there are a few areas in which you need to be clear. Laura and I developed a *Mentor Well: Quick Start Guide for PhD Advisors* that was part of a larger project for the Council of Graduate Schools (Lunsford & Baker, 2015). What I outline here is adapted from that Quick Start Guide.

First, what are your area(s) of need? These areas might be related to how to handle difficult or disengaged departmental colleagues or you might need help actively carving out time to finish a book project you started months before. Be clear on your needs to ensure you are seeking the "right" mentor(s); clarity also helps guide the conversation with a prospective mentor about your need and how you think the prospective mentor can help. Second, make a list of your top five must-haves/can't stands when engaged in a mentoring relationship or any working relationship for that matter. What has and has not worked well for you in the past and why? What are your related expectations and how do you like to work in a mentorship? You need to be thoughtful about what has, and has not, worked in the past and be explicit about creating a mentorship that meets your needs.

Third, ask yourself—what is my work style and what work style(s) best align with mine? Throughout my career, I have learned (sometimes the hard way) which approaches to work complement mine, and which ones are just frustrating to manage beyond in short doses. The same applies to mentorships. I genuinely enjoy my mentors and reaching out to them for guidance brings relief, not panic or dread. I know that I will feel better after interacting with any of my mentors, and I will have some direction to help me address an issue I am facing. Finally, you must be clear about the expectations you have of your mentor(s) and associated expectations you have for yourself as a mentee. Tell them what does and does not work for you.

Be clear about the type of support needed and ask directly if the mentor feels equipped, capable, and willing to provide it. Use this conversation to ask your mentor to communicate their expectations of you and how they engage as a mentor. This two-way relationship must be built on trust, honesty, and communication to be effective. Bottom line—Do not be afraid to be honest about your needs and expectations. Do not be afraid to walk away if those needs and expectations cannot be met. There are other mentors out there that will complement and meet your needs, and they too will benefit by engaging as a mentor in the process. Also, be sure you are fulfilling your responsibilities in the mentorship. If you are not, own it and do not be afraid to recalibrate.

Fostering effective mentorships takes time, and you need to be willing to invest that time and uphold your responsibilities in the mentorship. As you think about the individuals who might serve as effective mentors, I encourage you to reach out and schedule a meeting or virtually connect to learn more about each other and to talk about your needs and reasons for reaching out. Also, do not be afraid to ask a peer or colleague to facilitate an introduction with a prospective mentor. This can help alleviate anxiety you might have about making that first contact. I have done this for many colleagues, and I have asked others to do the same on my behalf. Through those initial interactions you will be able to determine if this person has the potential to be an effective mentor, and you can begin to gauge their willingness to serve.

Other Strategies: Delegation

While the predominant focus in this chapter is to help you assemble and foster a team of mentors that support your growth and development, I offer a few other tips and tools in this section that will be useful to you. As department chairs, time is precious and is frankly a commodity. I cannot add more hours to your day, but I can help you be more efficient with your time as you develop critical management and leadership skills (see Chapter 5). One of the most important skills you can foster is delegation, which helps you manage your time more effectively and serves as a professional development opportunity for others in your department.

Delegate, delegate, delegate. I assume by now, you have learned that you cannot do everything yourself, or at least not at a high quality over a sustained period of time. Every effective leader and manager has developed the learned skill to delegate responsibilities to team members. Delegation helps you manage your tasks and responsibilities while engaging others in the advancement of your department by providing them with an opportunity to take ownership, thus enhancing their related skills and competencies. Delegation can be hard, especially for those Type A personalities, but you have to trust your peers that they are capable, with support, of rising to the occasion.

There are many resources available to help you master the skill of delegation, including determining what you should and should not delegate. The article, *15 Effective Delegation Strategies for Busy Leaders* notes, "In order to avoid burnout and declining productivity, it's important to delegate certain tasks to trusted employees" (Forbes Coaches Council, 2019, para 2). Three strategies stand out to me that are particularly apropos for department chairs. First, choose one thing to delegate. This task could be assigning a departmental colleague as liaison for admissions events and coordinating departmental representation or serving as the point of contact with the office of sponsored research who must stay abreast of related happenings and sharing those with colleagues. Whatever the task or role you are delegating, the entire aspect of the task must be delegated. Second, find the hungry team members who are eager to sharpen their skills and take on a more visible leadership role in your department and the institution pending the responsibility or role delegated. Third, set clear expectations up front. Identifying and communicating expectations is fundamental to establishing an environment built on trust and account-ability. Communicate expectations often and do not be afraid to assess expectations with regularity and revise if needed.

Creating an environment and culture of shared departmental respon-sibility takes time. However, that investment is well spent given effective delegation helps foster a sense of commitment, community, and peer accountability. Further, it gives you the space you need to pursue your career and personal goals while training the next department chair in your department.

Chapter Summary and Next Steps

Serving as the department chair provides an invaluable service to both your department and institution. The responsibilities, tasks, and actions you engage in daily are many and are vital to ensuring departmental fac-ulty, staff, and students' needs are well-served. Nevertheless, that service often comes at a cost, namely in terms of your own career advancement and engagement in the professional endeavors you find personally and professionally meaningful (and that are necessary to help you advance in your career). Bottom line—just because you are department chair and are tasked with supporting others, does not mean you no longer need support and mentorship. It is this reality that serves as the motivation behind the featured problem in this chapter—**limited access to mentors to support your career advancement while serving as department chair**.

For many academics, mentoring has played a vital role in their profes-sional and personal development and aided them in their success to date. However, the mentoring strategies employed early in one's career will likely not serve mid-career academics as successfully as they had prior; this is especially true for those serving as department chairs given the trium-virate of leadership, management, and personnel development responsi-bilities that accompany this role. Building a mentoring network becomes paramount to both help you be successful across your department chair responsibilities while also advancing your own professional and personal goals and aspirations. Knowing the critical elements of mentoring at mid-career, learning how to manage mentoring at mid-career, and using the associated tools such as the mentoring needs inventory presented in this chapter will provide the guidance you need as department chair. Further, employing the delegation strategies noted will help you create space to foster the mentoring network you need to advance.

In the final chapters of this book, I turn my attention to institutional-level considerations related to MCF development. Chapter 7 sheds light on diversifying the portfolio of faculty development supports that meet the needs of faculty. Specifically, the chapter makes a case about the importance of engaging in regular assessments of your faculty development portfolio, and provides steps to complete that assessment and to ensure programming meets the needs of your faculty.

References

Baker, V. L., Gonzales, L. D., & Terosky, A. L. (2020). Faculty-inspired strategies for early career success across institutional types: The role of mentoring. In I. J. Beverly, B. N. Jennifer, S. J. Linda, K. Frances, G. Ruben, A. Nahed (Eds.), *The Wiley international handbook of mentoring: paradigms, practices, programs, and possibilities* (pp. 223–241). Wiley Blackwell.

Baker, V. L., & Manning, C. E. (2021). A mid-career faculty agenda: A review of four decades of research and practice. *Higher Education: Handbook of Theory and Research, 36*, 419.

Curran, W., Hamilton, T., Mansfield, B., Mountz, A., Walton-Roberts, M., Werner, M., & Whitson, R. (2019). "Will you be my mentor?" Feminist mentoring at mid-career for institutional change. *Gender, Place & Culture, 26*(12), 1721–1739.

Dickens M. & Gademer, K. (2018). The benefits of mid-career mentoring. *American Planning Association blog.* www.planning.org/blog/blogpost/9151503/

Flaherty, C. (2016, December 1). Forgotten chairs. *Inside HigherEd.* www.insidehighered.com/news/2016/12/01/new-study-suggests-training-department-chairs-woefully-inadequate-most-institutions

Forbes Coaches Council (2019, November 18). 15 effective delegation strategies for busy leaders. *Forbes.* www.forbes.com/sites/forbescoachescouncil/2019/11/18/15-effective-delegation-strategies-for-busy-leaders/?sh=100b78784e36

Gmelch, W. H. (1991). Paying the price for academic leadership: Department chair tradeoffs. *Educational Record, 72*(3), 45–49.

Gmelch, W. H. (2002). *The call for department leaders.* [Research paper presentation]. Annual Meeting of the American Association of College Teacher Education, February 23–26, New York, NY.

Gmelch, W. H. (2015). The call for leadership: Why chairs serve, what they do, and how long they should serve. *AKA Monographs: Leading and Managing the Kinesiology Department, 1*(1), 1–12.

Goldsmith, M. (2010). *What got you here won't get you there: How successful people become even more successful.* Profile books.

Higgins, M. C., & Kram, K. E. (2001). Reconceptualizing mentoring at work: A developmental network perspective. *Academy of Management Review*, 26(2), 264–288.

Jackson, J. F. L. (2019, March 19). To chair, or not to chair? *The Chronicle of Higher Education*. www.chronicle.com/article/to-chair-or-not-to-chair/?cid2= gen_login_refresh&cid=gen_sign_in

Johnson, W. B. (2015). *On being a mentor: A guide for higher education faculty*. Routledge.

Johnson, W. B., & Ridley, C. R. (2018). *The elements of mentoring: 75 practices of master mentors*. St. Martin's Press.

Johnson, W. B., & Smith, D. (2016). *Athena rising: How and why men should mentor women*. New York: Routledge.

Law, A. V., Bottenberg, M. M., Brozick, A. H., Currie, J. D., DiVall, M. V., Haines, S. T., & Yablonski, E. (2014). A checklist for the development of faculty mentorship programs. *American Journal of Pharmaceutical Education*, 78(5), 1–10.

List, K., & Sorcinelli, M. D. (2018). Increasing leadership capacity for senior women faculty through mutual mentoring. *The Journal of Faculty Development*, 32(1), 7–16.

Lunsford, L. G., & Baker, V. (2015). Great mentoring in graduate school: A quick start guide for protégés. *Council for Graduate Schools*. https://cgsnet. org/ckfinder/userfiles/files/CGS_OPS_Mentoring2016.pdf

Lunsford, L. G. (2016). *A handbook for managing mentoring programs: Starting, supporting and sustaining*. Routledge.

Lunsford, L., Crisp, G., Dolan, E., Wuetherick, B., (2017). *Mentoring in higher education*. In D. A. Clutterbuck, F. K. Cochan, L. G. Lunsford, N. Dominguez, & J. Haddock-Millar (Eds.), *The SAGE handbook of mentoring* (pp. 316–334). Sage Publications.

Lunsford, L. G (2020). Mapping your mentoring network. In V. L. Baker (Ed.), *Charting your path to full: A guide for women associate professors* (pp. 136–161). Rutgers University Press.

O'Connor, G. (2004). *Miracle*. Walt Disney Pictures and Mayhem Pictures.

Ouellette, C. M. (2020, October 27). A chair's life in 3 stages. *Inside HigherEd*. www.insidehighered.com/advice/2020/10/27/insights-new-department-chair-has-gained-during-pandemic-opinion

Rashid, B. (2017, May 2). 3 reasons all great leaders have mentors (and mentees). *Forbes*.   www.forbes.com/sites/brianrashid/2017/05/02/3-reasons-all-great-leaders-have-mentors-and-mentees/?sh=2ac7012313f9

Reddick, R. J. (2019, 2020). *Mid-career mentoring*. Handout shared at the annual meetings of the Association for the Study of Higher Education and the American Educational Research Association.

Sorcinelli, M. D., & Yun, J. (2007). From mentor to mentoring networks: Mentoring in the new academy. *Change: The Magazine of Higher Learning*, 39(6), 58–61.

Willingham-McLain, L., Margolis, J., & Klingler, N. (2019). Designing and evaluating a near-peer mentoring exchange for early-career faculty. *The Journal of Faculty Development*, 33(3), 59–70.

Chapter 7

Assessing and Investing in Your Faculty Development Portfolio

Francis has been the dean of faculty at a research institution for 18 months. Prior to this role, she was a full professor in the social sciences. Francis felt confident in assuming the deanship, considering her experience as department chair and committee chair of both personnel and faculty development committees. As a faculty member, she recalls the challenges she faced when advancing along her career noting, "sexism was certainly at play" in addition to gendered work norms, "which still rear their ugly head." Despite being resource constrained, Francis does consider her budget robust enough to offer some strong faculty development programming throughout the academic year with summer offerings every other year. She recently met with the provost to argue the need to enhance her budget in order to expand her existing offerings. The provost was receptive to the idea and requested Francis prepare a presentation that highlighted various related outcomes such as number of programs, types/content of programs, and attendance (including the total number of attendees and disciplines represented). Based on the information Francis presented, it was clear that early career faculty at her institution were being served well despite room for improvement. Program topics addressed critical needs to advance toward tenure and promotion and there was a diversity of offerings. Yet, as Francis was preparing her presentation she realized how few programs were targeted to mid- and late-career stage colleagues, and the ones that are offered are not well attended. One of the reasons she pursued this position was to change this reality, knowing how challenging mid-career can be. The extra funding she was seeking would go directly to developing and delivering programs that would benefit those beyond early career. Yet, the conversation with the provost did not go as planned. While he

DOI: 10.4324/9781003201311-10

agreed with the importance of supports that were specific to faculty career stage, he did not believe the data was compelling enough to increase her budget, especially when budget cuts were being made across other academic areas. Instead, Francis was encouraged to "re-evaluate the existing programs to see where you can make adjustments."

Francis' situation is not unique to research institutions. All institution types must be thoughtful about how, and in what ways, they invest in faculty development programming and related supports. Some institutions want to ensure that there is a strong return on that investment leading to an evaluation of associated outcomes and corresponding metrics. As we have discussed throughout this book, a wealth of programming and resources are available to early career colleagues on a per-institution basis and broadly across the field of higher education. While increasing over the past 15 years, there are still fewer programs and resources targeted toward mid-career faculty (MCF) compared to their early career peers (Baker & Manning, 2021; Baldwin, 2005). One contributing factor is the cost and resources needed to broaden institutional faculty development portfolios to meet this need, knowing the needs of MCF are quite diverse (Strage & Merdiger, 2015). Another contributing factor is engagement, or lack thereof, in the mid-career programming that does exist (Baker et al., 2017).

Throughout our research, and that of others, administrators have acknowledged the importance of MCF programming; MCF members have communicated their eagerness to engage in such programming (Baker, 2019; Baker et al., 2016; Flaherty, 2017). Yet, there was still a disconnect. What we found is the featured problem of this chapter: **Existing faculty development programming does not meet the needs of seasoned faculty or the institutions that employ them**. I truly believe campus leaders, administrators, and faculty developers are committed to providing needed supports, resources, and programming to their MCF. In addition, I believe a majority of MCF will invest their time and energy in engaging in faculty programming *if* the programming meets their needs, regardless of their career aspirations. The COVID-19 pandemic has both heightened existing needs of faculty members while surfacing others. Now, more than ever, it is imperative to invest in faculty development supports, but that investment needs to be strategic in order to benefit faculty members and their institutions. I see this as an exciting opportunity in the academy.

The aim of this chapter is to highlight MCF needs, particularly as driven by context (e.g., career stage, discipline) and around leadership development, formal and informal. By narrowing in on those areas, faculty development scholars and practitioners can help advance programming at the institutional level to ensure the right investments are being directed toward the right programs. To support that goal, I walk you through the Faculty Development Portfolio Assessment and pulse-taking survey tools. My hope is to help support you in your work as an institutional leader tasked with advancing a faculty development agenda.

What Do Mid-Career Faculty Need and Want?

Throughout my research and practice, I have seen and heard similar comments about existing faculty development offerings. Comments from MCF sound something like: "The programs never change," "My needs are different now," and "I'll attend when the programming actually provides a value add." Faculty developers and other campus administrators lament, "The same five or six faculty show up every time," "We are spending a great deal of resources with little, visible reward," and "I cannot justify the expense." I have always found it disheartening that these sentiments are shared on the same campus, confirming a lack of communication or deliberateness about how to meet MCF members' needs while investing resources wisely. I ask one simple question when I bring stakeholders from these two groups together—have you talked collaboratively about how to better meet MCF members' needs with the resources available? The answer is often "no." These conversations are not happening as regularly as they should be, if at all.

While I am a big advocate for capacity-building and open communication in relation to faculty development programming (see Chapter 8), all one needs to do is turn to the literature and related practice on MCF to identify a starting point to help identify what MCF need and want. The most comprehensive resource, at present, is the meta-synthesis my colleague and I prepared for *Higher Education: Handbook of Theory and Research* (Baker & Manning, 2021). We conducted a review across four decades of literature and identified the trends that were present within and across those decades. It is that analysis that informs the themes presented in this chapter. If you are an institutional leader or plan on being one in the future, I strongly encourage you to think about programming that addresses and or accounts for the following: Leadership development and context.

Leadership Development

If your faculty development portfolio does not include leadership development programming, individual and group-based, you are doing your faculty and your institution a disservice. Simply put, "faculty leadership is necessary for high-quality teaching, innovative curriculum, cutting-edge research, intellectual enrichment, student engagement, improved student outcomes, greater faculty citizenship, a more democratic environment, a campus more responsive to community needs, and other important outcomes" (Kezar et al., 2007, p. 21). Leadership development initiatives should be aimed at early career faculty in order to ensure the skills and competencies needed to be successful in later career stages are developed. However, at minimum, leadership development targeted at mid-career should be a staple in your career development portfolio (Baker & Manning, inpress; Kiel, 2015).

I offer a few leadership considerations to help inform your related thinking and program development. First, be clear on how leadership is defined on your campus. When we hear the term "leadership," we often think of those occupying formal roles such as chair, director, unit head, or dean. Those who occupy such roles need formal training and onboarding to ensure they are equipped to meet the needs of the organization and to advance professionally and personally while serving in these formal roles. However, such training should start before someone assumes such a role. As Cano and Whitfield (2019) so aptly noted, the academy is in need of talent that is presently ready or poised to be ready to assume new positions, which they refer to as "bench strength." As we all learned from the COVID-19 pandemic, our environment as we know it can change in a moment's notice. We need competent, capable individuals ready to jump in when called upon or to rise to the occasion if already in the role.

Second, leadership also happens across higher education in informal ways, and informal leadership contributions need to be recognized and fostered. Faculty, for example, regularly serve as mentors to students and peers and as exemplars of effective teaching. Faculty are visible community-engaged leaders serving as bridges between their local community and institution. Such leadership is vital to the success of our institutions and needs to be elevated to the appropriate level. Ask yourself, what programs does my institution offer that support and recognize leadership in the following areas: Teaching, scholarship, service, mentoring, advocacy, and community-based learning? If the program and resource list is short across these areas, you have now identified a starting point for defining what leadership, formal and informal, means on your campus and the spaces and contexts in which it occurs.

Context

Let me say this for the people in the back—context matters! Moreover, several contexts should inform your faculty development programming. First, discipline and disciplinary differences should factor into your MCF development planning (actually, disciplinary differences should influence programming across all career stages). Accounting for academic division is crucial because a "faculty members' academic home or discipline is the location in which faculty learning occurs predominantly and disciplinary knowledge is developed" (Baker et al., 2018, p. 1337). Norms about collaboration, author order, learning environments, methodologies, pedagogical approaches, and work styles are driven by discipline. This means, for example, you should host divisional sessions focused on preparing for full professorship in which successful faculty from that divisional area share their experiences. Additionally, current and former members of the personnel committee should offer insights based on "lessons learned" and as informed from their review experiences serving on the committee. You might also host leadership development sessions for aspiring leaders on your campus titled, "Leadership in the Humanities: How to Develop Your Skills." Again, this is about building your "bench strength" as Cano and Whitfield (2019) argued.

Second, institutional context needs to be visible and accounted for in faculty development programming. While this statement seems so obvious, you would be surprised at how few institutions really account for this context as part of their portfolio of career development offerings. I say this because many institutions have continued to increase performance standards and expectations in regards to faculty workload, yet their faculty development programming and corresponding resources have failed to evolve at the same pace. I see this a great deal in community colleges and liberal arts colleges, even comprehensive institutions to an extent in relation to scholarly and creative activity given expectations are on the rise across these institution types, domestic and abroad while teaching expectations have not changed (Kyvik, 2013). In fact, performance expectations are increasing across all areas of faculty workload, regardless of institution type (Strawser, 2020), and faculty are in need of support. This reality in the academy informs the tools and resources offered in this chapter as institutional leaders and faculty developers are charged with supporting their faculty with limited resources to do so.

Third, the changing nature of higher education requires support and resources to help faculty manage these changes, particularly the ones they "see" every day in their interactions with students and peers. A diversifying student population, increased mental health needs of students, and greater enrollment of first-generation and non-traditional student populations means you need to equip faculty with the tools, resources, and campus and community contacts to provide the needed support to students (Anderson, 2020). As St. Amour shared, "Getting faculty to adapt to the times takes planning, buy-in and, most importantly, money" (2020, para 14). Expecting faculty to rise to the occasion without dedicated supports and deliberateness informing those supports is misinformed, at best. We have all heard the saying before: It takes a village to support a student; it also takes a village to support faulty members who are on the front lines with students day in and day out.

In closing, faculty development is an investment of time and resources and requires constant care and engagement. A one-size-fits-all approach to faculty development is not just antiquated; it is detrimental to attracting, retaining, and supporting the advancement and engagement of your faculty. You have an opportunity to innovate and diversify your career development portfolio, which *is* as a differentiator and sends a message about what you value and how your institution lives those values. I am rooting for you as you create your faculty development village that fosters diverse partnerships and communities in which learning, growth, and contributions are valued and supported. Your faculty will appreciate the support; your institution will thrive.

Returning to Francis' Experience

Francis is an excellent example of a faculty member whose experience inspired an interest and willingness to serve her institution as an upper-level administrator and leader. She is a woman faculty member who advanced through the academic ranks, having earned full professorship. She also occupied several leadership positions and has contributed to faculty governance in myriad ways. Throughout those experiences, she realized there was an opportunity to do more at her institution to support faculty as they move along the professoriate. Francis also was confident in her belief that investing in faculty throughout their careers would benefit her institution. Yet, her challenge was figuring out how to continue to meet the needs of those faculty members who are being served, while creating space and securing resources that would allow for the broadening of existing programming. This dilemma is not unique to Francis or her institution. All institutional leaders and faculty developers grapple with this issue regularly. Rather than view this as a challenge, Francis (and I) view this as a unique opportunity to contribute in meaningful ways.

As we return to Francis' experience described in the opening case, put yourself in her shoes. What strategy would you employ to help persuade your provost of the importance to increase faculty development funding? Or, perhaps you put yourself in the position of Francis' provost. What data do you need to see or outcomes do you need to learn about to justify increasing faculty development expenditures? Write down your thoughts in the space provided as we dive into the key details of the case.

_____

_____

_____

_____

_____

_____
_____
_____
_____
_____
_____
_____
_____
_____
_____
_____
_____
_____
_____
_____
_____
_____
_____

Relevant Facts

We know that Francis is a full professor having served as a faculty member in the social sciences. We also know that Francis has occupied several leadership positions on her campus having served as department chair and as a member (and chair) of faculty focused campus committees. Her experiences in these various roles inspired her to pursue a senior leadership position on her campus charged with supporting faculty. Francis' own experiences as a faculty member were not without challenges; sexism and gendered worker norms were present and still are, based on her assessment and those of her women academic peers. Francis hoped to "move the needle" on these issues, realizing she needs to work from the institutional level down and hoping her efforts permeate across her campus.

She has occupied the role of dean of faculty for 18 months and has found that early career faculty are being served, acknowledging that there is always room for improvement. Where programming is lacking, however, is at the MCF (and beyond) stages. She knows she needs to secure additional funding to broaden the programs offered, but she also knows funding across her institution is tight making this request even more challenging. In her words, "I know the provost agrees with me in theory about the importance of investing in faculty beyond early career. I am just not sure if he supports this belief in practice as evidenced by increased funding."

Key Stakeholders

Francis has two primary stakeholders she must keep on the forefront of her planning and related efforts: The provost and faculty on her campus, specifically MCF (of which she herself is one despite having earned full professor). Francis said she has a "good working relationship with the provost" and believes him to be a "reasonable and fair" campus leader. However, she also notes that he is not always as transparent as he could be or is as preferred by individuals across campus. She knows the provost is mostly persuaded by data, not anecdotes.

Francis is also faced with the dilemma of continuing to serve early career faculty effectively while increasing the available programming and resources targeted toward MCF. Shifting resources (e.g., financial, programming, time allocated to training and development) to mid-career programming inevitably means less going toward early career faculty. Combining resources is an option, but Francis also realizes the importance of creating safe spaces for early career faculty to express concerns and to share their experiences in rooms that do not include senior colleagues. MCF also prefer to not divulge professional (or personal) details in front of early career colleagues or those who are more senior.

Needed Information

Francis understands the budget she is working with and she has been responsible for managing the portfolio of offerings since assuming the position 18 months ago. She needs greater clarity, however, on the types of programs that would benefit MCF. In order to do that, she knows she needs to either secure existing data or collect her own to paint a more concrete picture of the experiences of MCF across her institution. She needs to know how well, or not, those faculty are being served.

Francis also needs to determine what other funding options exist beyond the provost simply increasing her budget. Francis needs to find out, for example, if there are opportunities to partner with Institutional Advancement and Development, foundations, or alumni who want to invest in faculty. Francis can also explore other strategies for capacity building through offices and units across campus, through consortiums of which her institution is a member, or colleagues through professional associations with related expertise. She knows she is not able to develop and deliver all the needed programming herself; securing partners to help her advance her agenda will be necessary.

Lastly, Francis needs to engage in strategic planning to more clearly articulate her vision, as informed by data and faculty need with accompanying short, medium, and long-term targets. She knows that the first new programs that she offers need to be a success, which will help her leverage future resources. She also needs to be strategic in determining which MCF programs will result in the greatest outcomes at the individual, departmental, and institution levels.

Case Summary

Francis is approaching her role and responsibility as dean of faculty in a thoughtful way, yet she knows her approach must be deliberate if she plans to advance and innovate faculty development programing on her campus. She realized rather quickly that while useful, her personal and professional experiences and observations alone will not help her advance her agenda; she needs support from a variety of partners interested in supporting and advancing faculty at her institution.

During our initial conversation, it became clear that Francis needed coaching to refine her strategy and support execution. We agreed to collaborate and committed to six coaching sessions throughout the academic year, and we outlined Francis' goal: To re-pitch the faculty development plan to her provost *including* other key campus stakeholders in order to secure needed funding. First, she needed compelling data to illustrate *who* was serving faculty, *how* faculty were being served (or not), *who* among the faculty were being served, and *how* existing faculty development programming achieved the aims established for faculty performance (or not) as outlined in their faculty handbook. One of Francis' professional goals was to elevate her presence on campus. Our focus on capacity building to advance her faculty development programming agenda is one way to achieve that goal and provided her with a unique opportunity to engage with individuals and programs across campus.

Tools, Strategies, and Resources

As I shared earlier in the book, you need to know where you currently are in order to get to where you want to be. Situating this motto in the context of the featured problem in this chapter, institutional leaders need to be clear about (1) who or which units/departments have faculty development responsibility; (2) communicated (e.g., written) faculty performance expectations; and (3) the programming and resources available to faculty members to assist their professional growth and advancement. Without this knowledge, you will not be able to support faculty or advance your institution in the ways you intend. To that end, I walk you through what I refer to as the Faculty Development Portfolio Assessment. There are three core components to this assessment, and I describe each in the next section.

Faculty Development Portfolio Assessment

Faculty development programming and related resources are an investment, and for some institutions, this can be a significant expenditure. Investment is defined as the action of allocating money or resources to realize a profit or material result. In higher education, we do not expect to "earn money" by investing in faculty development programs and resources. Instead, the goal is to see some type of material result such as faculty skill development and enhancement with implications at the student, faculty, department, and institutional levels. In order to benefit from the material result, you need to make the right investments, and that requires constant care, attention, and review to ensure resources are used wisely. It is important to remember, the higher education landscape has changed over the last five years, and especially so during the pandemic, which might have accelerated how antiquated some faculty development programs are now. You need to be willing to ask the right, sometime tough questions, and adjust accordingly.

Component 1. The first component of the Faculty Development Portfolio Assessment involves identifying all the individuals, committees, and units, departments, and centers that have faculty development responsibility. This may include, but is not limited to, the provost or academic dean, dean or associate dean of faculty, faculty advocate, the faculty personnel committee, the faculty development committee, the center for teaching and learning, or the office of sponsored research.

In the space provided below, list each individual and every entity that might be connected to faculty development and describe their primary charge using an estimated percentage (e.g., provost = 20% time devoted to faculty development). Note this detail will come in handy as we work through building a communication strategy in Chapter 8. For now, knowing who has responsibility and their primary charge supports this aspect of the Faculty Development Portfolio Assessment. Take a moment and start drafting your list now.

_____

_____

_____

_____

_____

_____

_____

_____
_____
_____
_____
_____
_____
_____
_____
_____
_____
_____
_____
_____
_____
_____

After developing your list, consider sharing it with colleagues and others on campus who have insight into faculty development. Francis found this to be an important professional development exercise in advancing her own agenda as dean of faculty. She realized she was not clear in terms of all the individuals and entities who engaged in faculty development in various capacities. She shared her list with a few colleagues engaged in faculty development work to ensure its accuracy. Completing this step of the assessment helped her think about ways to streamline existing efforts and resources; she was also able to forge relationships with units to enhance existing offerings that, with minor adjustments, could benefit a wider audience, thus expanding programs and resources available (with no change to her budget).

Component 2. The second component includes writing out the faculty performance expectations formally communicated in your institution's faculty handbook or some other institutional artifact. Ask your-self, what are the areas in which faculty are expected to be excellent across teaching, scholarship, and service? Your institution might have additional categories or these categories may look slightly different at promotion and tenure versus advancement to full. Regardless, these cri-teria need to be front and center in your Faculty Development Portfolio Assessment. Be sure to include specific details. For example, if mentoring is important, be sure to note that, and include details about the contexts in which mentoring is expected to occur. Or if an international reputation is important for advancement to full, be sure to note that detail. Include both the formal, written expectations, and the informal, "in practice" expectations that surface. Engaging members of the faculty personnel committee in conversation about what they look for and how they conduct their review of dossiers will be useful. Again, take a moment to look up the criteria and list them out, including descriptions of the criteria that are formally communicated.

_____

_____

_____

_____

_____

_____

_____

_____

_____

_____

_____

_____

_____

_____

_____

_____

_____

_____

_____

_____

_____

_____

_____

_____

_____

_____

It is the informal, "in practice" aspects that Francis found most alarming. After engaging current and former members of the faculty personnel committee, she found out that expectations of what is considered acceptable and "expected of faculty" have evolved. Yet, the handbook language did not mirror that reality. The "in practice" was more realistic in terms of present day faculty expectations based on knowledge gleaned from the conversations Francis hosted and feedback shared with faculty as they engaged in advancement processes. In fact, there was a disconnect between how faculty were being evaluated across some areas and what was communicated in the handbook. This was certainly an area in which Francis needed to make some headway.

Component 3. Third, create a visual inventory of the first two components, mapping out who has responsibility for what. For example, if faculty are expected to be "excellent teachers" ask yourself: What resources, programs, and tools are available to faculty and who is responsible for developing, delivering, and assessing those programs? How many of those programs and resources account for career stage and discipline/division to help faculty achieve this aim? Additionally, if faculty are expected to engage in scholarly and creative activities, what resources, programs, and tools are available to help faculty achieve this aim, again accounting for career stage and discipline/divisional differences and needs? Who has responsibility for providing this support and ensuring that support meets faculty members' needs?

This exercise can be as simple as creating a table in which the headings are the handbook language criteria; the rows are the various individuals and/or committees that have faculty development responsibility. See Table 7.1 for an example of the visual Francis and I worked through.

To start, simply put an "X" in the boxes to create a visual representation of programs and resources offered and who has primary responsibility for developing, delivering, and evaluating those programs to ensure they are meeting faculty members' and institutional needs. This is a powerful exercise to help you identify where there are disconnects between what is expected of faculty and the resources available to ensure they are able to meet those expectations.

Once you have the visual, you can now create a more detailed inventory of the programs included. Key information to list includes the title of program, population(s) served, frequency and cost of the program, assessment data (who attends including discipline and career stage, satisfaction with program), who offers the program, and the goal(s) of program. If you are not regularly collecting this data, you now have a

Table 7.1 Sample Faculty Development Portfolio Assessment Table

	Teaching	Scholarship/Creative Activity	Service
Faculty Development Committee		X	
Faculty Personnel Committee		X	
Center for Teaching & Learning	X		
Instructional Technology	X		
Department Chairs			
Faculty Steering Committee			
Provost's Office	X		

good starting place. In the space provided, either start writing down the corresponding details for your inventory of programs and/or map out plans for how you plan to start collecting this data in future programming.

_____

_____

_____

_____

_____

_____

_____

_____

_____

_____

_____

_____

_____

_____

_____

_____

_____

_____

_____

_____

_____

_____

_____

_____

_____

_____

_____

_____

_____

_____

_____

_____

_____

_____

_____

_____

_____

Working through the third component of the Faculty Development Portfolio Assessment revealed a few key points of information for Francis. First, she and her institution did not have all the data about each program outlined here. This information, she realized, was critical for decision-making and resource allocation purposes. Our goal was to be intentional and targeted with resources available, in order to leverage resources needed. Second, Francis' office, as well as other departments on campus, did a good job of supporting faculty in their scholarly and creative efforts, which was not entirely surprising given the institutional mission. The majority of those programs were targeted toward early career faculty. There was still more opportunities to support faculty across career stages in this area. Teaching, while present and supported through their center for teaching and learning, was not as balanced as it needed to be; however, Francis was hopeful given the wealth of resources and support made available during the COVID-19 pandemic, particularly around online teaching. There was no formal, sustained leadership training beyond a weekend workshop for newly appointed department chairs; no training was offered for committee chairs and other formal faculty roles (e.g., faculty liaison). Limited sessions focused on supporting faculty members in their service (e.g., faculty governance) or to advance skills in community-engaged learning or mentoring, for example.

In summary, this new knowledge coupled with understanding from research and practice enabled Francis to design an action plan on where to focus her efforts. Her time was limited given her administrative role as dean while also still engaging in her discipline, as well as her personal responsibilities as a mother of two. As a result of our coaching sessions, including the faculty development portfolio assessment and development of pulse-taking surveys, we identified three priorities for the upcoming academic year to enhance her existing faculty development portfolio. Those priorities focused on capacity-building, increasing clarity on who is responsible for what to reduce redundancies and inefficiencies, and creating the needed infrastructure to support program development, delivery, and assessment. With those priorities in mind, Francis hosted faculty focus groups by career stage and division to learn more about faculty members' needs and challenges to help inform program development. I also encouraged her to use pulse-taking surveys, which I describe next.

Pulse-Taking Survey

A pulse-taking survey is a short survey lasting a maximum of five minutes sent to employees on a regular basis as a "pulse check" to determine how things are going. Using targeted questions, topics can cover overall employee satisfaction, job expectations, communication, and work environment. Using such a data collection technique assists with developing and sustaining employee engagement, outcomes critical to individuals and the organizations that employ them (Society for Human Resource Management, 2021).

Given her goal of supporting faculty, Francis needed to engage faculty regularly in low cost, efficient ways that provide valuable, timely insights. I recommended that Francis start administering pulse surveys on targeted topics around career stage and disciplinary needs of faculty. I suggested she use the pulse surveys to assess the current state, to inform future state resource allocation decisions, and to facilitate more regular interaction and communication with faculty that would not burden their schedules. The data from the pulse surveys would provide her with valuable information that would be easier to analyze and act on compared to a longer, more in-depth workplace surveys. For example, the first pulse survey Francis sent to faculty included one simple question—"If you have time to attend only one professional development workshop or seminar this year, what topic would that session address?" This data, coupled with knowledge gleaned from the Faculty Development Portfolio Assessment, enabled Francis to advance her agenda and support the faculty at her institution. Spoiler alert—Francis recently presented findings to her provost and he has agreed to increase her budget by 5%; she also is working with institutional advancement on fundraising initiatives to support program development and delivery.

It bears repeating—in order to get to where you want to go, you need to have a clear understanding of where you currently stand. Faculty development, and the associated investments that support programming, are too critical to advancing faculty and the institutions that employ them to not invest the time and energy in regular assessment and review. Faculty populations, needs, and challenges evolve over time and so must your faculty development programming. As an institutional leader, you have an opportunity to be creative and innovative, to illustrate to current and prospective faculty the value you place in faculty and the ways in which you support their contributions. The Faculty Development Portfolio Assessment described here will get you on your way!

Chapter Summary and Next Steps

Faculty members are vital to the success of their institutions. Thriving engaged faculty members means a thriving, innovative institution. In order to foster individual and organizational thriving, however, it requires thoughtful, sustained investment in the human capital of the organization. I am sincere when I say that I do believe the majority of campus leaders and faculty developers are committed to investing in their faculty members; I also truly believe a majority of faculty are interested in growing, developing, learning, and contributing to their institutions in order to see it succeed. Nevertheless, thriving and success do not happen overnight or without intentionality. I find it so disheartening when faculty and campus leaders are more aligned then they realize when it comes to the types of support needed across the stages of the faculty career, yet existing faculty development programming does not meet the needs of seasoned faculty or the institutions that employ them, the featured problem in this chapter.

I do believe part of the issue lies in not knowing how to tackle this problem effectively or efficiently. My goal in this chapter, and in writing this book for that matter, is to provide MCF members, department chairs, and institutional leaders with tools and resources that help them advance their professional agendas while also advancing the aims of their institutions. The Faculty Development Portfolio Assessment and pulse-taking survey are two tools that can aid in this process. By using these tools, campus leaders and administrators gather critical data to inform program development and delivery and well as resource allocation. In addition, they open the lines of communication between two critical campus stakeholders—the administration and faculty.

In fact, communication is the focus of the final content chapter of this book. In Chapter 8, I focus on the importance of communicating the types of faculty programs and resources available to faculty. Through my consulting work, I have worked with campus leaders on campuses with a wealth of faculty development resources and tools, yet knowledge about those offerings and resources is limited. In Chapter 8, I highlight strategies to employ that open up the lines of communication to elevate the role faculty development can (and should) play on your campus.

References

Anderson, G. (2020, September 22). Mental health needs rise with the pandemic. *Inside HigherEd*. www.insidehighered.com/news/2020/09/11/students-great-need-mental-health-support-during-pandemic

Baker, V. L., Pifer, M. J., & Lunsford, L. G. (2016). Faculty challenges across rank in liberal arts colleges: A human resources perspective. *The Journal of Faculty Development, 30*(1), 23–30.

Baker, V. L., Lunsford, L. G., & Pifer, M. J. (2017). *Developing faculty in liberal arts colleges: Aligning individual needs and organizational goals*. Rutgers University Press.

Baker, V. L., Pifer, M. J., & Lunsford, L. G. (2018). Faculty development in liberal arts colleges: A look at divisional trends, preferences, and needs. *Higher Education Research & Development, 37*(7), 1336–1351.

Baker, V. L. (2019, January 30). Academe needs to take a cue from industry. *Inside HigherEd*. www.insidehighered.com/advice/2019/01/30/midcareer-faculty-members-need-more-training-and-development-opinion

Baker, V. L., & Manning, C. E. (2021). A mid-career faculty agenda: A review of four decades of research and practice. *Higher Education: Handbook of Theory and Research*, *36*, 419.

Baker. V. L. & Manning, C. E. N. (inpress). Preparing the Next Generation of Institutional Leaders: Strategic Supports for Mid-Career Faculty. *To Improve the Academy*.

Baldwin, R. G. (2005). Making mid-career meaningful. *The Department Chair*, *16*(2), 14–16.

Cano, A., & Whitfield, K. (2019, November, 22). Needed: Leadership training for faculty and academic staff. www.insidehighered.com/advice/2019/11/22/importance-cultivating-leadership-skills-among-faculty-and-academic-staff-members

Flaherty, C. (2017, January 26). Midcareer professors need love too. *Inside HigherEd*. www.insidehighered.com/news/2017/01/26/research-midcareer-professors-makes-case-support-after-tenure

Kezar, A., Lester, J., Carducci, R., Gallant, T. B., & McGavin, M. C. (2007). Where are the faculty leaders? Strategies and advice for reversing current trends. *Liberal Education*, *93*(4), 14–21.

Kiel, D. H. (2015). Creating a faculty leadership development program. *Academic Impressions*. www.academicimpressions.com/sites/default/files/1215-faculty-leadership-md.pdf

Kyvik, S. (2013). The academic researcher role: Enhancing expectations and improved performance. *Higher Education*, *65*(4), 525–538.

Society for Human Resource Management (2021). Developing and sustaining employee engagement. *SHRM*. www.shrm.org/resourcesandtools/tools-and-samples/toolkits/pages/sustainingemployeeengagement.aspx

St. Amour, M. (2020, April 3). As times and students change, can faculty change, too? *Inside HigherEd*. www.insidehighered.com/news/2020/04/03/faculty-face-uphill-battle-adapting-needs-todays-students

Strage, A., & Merdinger, J. (2015). Professional growth and renewal for mid-career faculty. *The Journal of Faculty Development*, *29*(1), 41–50.

Strawser, M. G. (2020, June 2). Navigating the new professoriate. *Inside HigherEd*. www.insidehighered.com/advice/2020/06/02/how-academic-administrators-can-help-faculty-handle-increased-expectations-while

Chapter 8

Organizing and Communicating
Getting Mid-Career Faculty Engaged

Matt is a full professor in STEM and serves as the director of his community college's center for faculty development where he has been employed for 15 years. Firmly a MCF member himself, he took on the director role to "switch things up professionally" and to "help his colleagues" advance in their careers. In his opinion, the faculty development offerings are fairly robust, especially given the resource constraints he and his institution must manage. And while the majority of their programs target early career faculty, he has worked hard the past two-and-a-half years to increase offerings targeted specifically towards MCF across their four divisions (natural sciences, social sciences, humanities, fine arts), and those programs have been well received. Nevertheless, Matt is still frustrated at the lack of MCF engagement in programs and related conversations. This is especially frustrating for Matt: "These programs are designed to help them and yet, I cannot get them to offer their feedback or to participate beyond one or two programs every couple years." Institutionally speaking, Matt also realizes their knowledge management systems leave a little to be desired, specifically having a system that tracks the faculty trajectory. Matt's goal is to develop a more sophisticated system that regularly monitors time in rank, performance/evaluation processes, and faculty members' experiences as they navigate these processes, and evaluative feedback shared with faculty, targeting the types of feedback shared with women and faculty of color. Ideally, Matt and other individuals on campus charged with faculty development responsibilities would meet regularly to review this data (if they had it), and this is something he laments about often. As he settles into this role, he has become aware that part of the problem is a lack of formal communication strategy; the other problem is not having the needed infrastructure to

DOI: 10.4324/9781003201311-11

better track progress, particularly for women and faculty of color, at his institution to support individually driven career development.

Does Matt's situation sound familiar to you? Alternatively, perhaps you are living Matt's reality regularly on your campus. You know you have solid faculty development programming on your campus, yet you know there is potential for that programming to benefit a wider faculty audience on your campus if only faculty would just participate. There is a disconnect, but you are not quite sure what that disconnect is or how to improve it. Unfortunately, I have heard, seen, and experienced this situation with regularity as a faculty member myself and as a consultant and academic coach working with institutional leaders and faculty members across the world. The problem is, **Existing institutional infrastructure does not highlight or promote faculty development programming**, the focus of this chapter, the final content chapter in this book.

In Chapter 7, I honed in on helping you build a robust, diverse portfolio of faculty development programming by walking you through a Faculty Development Portfolio Assessment. You now know where there are opportunities for growth based on faculty performance expectations as outlined in your faculty handbook; you also now know the faculty populations in need of better support. Knowledge gleaned from this assessment is aiding you as you work to advance these growth opportunities. However, you might still be frustrated by lack of engagement among your mid-career faculty (MCF), either in terms of participation in programming offered or by way of feedback (or lack thereof) as you work to plan future offerings. When my clients express these concerns, I usually ask the following questions: Are MCF aware of the programming and opportunities you offer? Moreover, are the available resources easily and intuitively accessible and career friendly? If you are unsure or answered no to either of these questions, the content in this chapter will help you address the disconnects you have found on your campus. I imagine there are fewer things more frustrating than actually having strong faculty-focused programming, yet your faculty are either unaware of what is available to them on and off your campus or they are unable to take advantage of what you offer.

In this chapter, I highlight two critical considerations that are necessary to support your faculty development efforts—communication and access. If either of these are absent or lacking, you will struggle to garner the type of engagement and benefits from your programming that you envision. These two concepts ground the literature review in the following section and inform the tools, strategies, and resources featured later in this chapter.

Communication and Access: Critical Considerations to Support Faculty Development

Once institutional leaders and faculty developers overcome the first barrier to faculty engagement in career development programming (e.g., lack of targeted programming that spans career stage and discipline), they must overcome the second hurdle—consistent faculty participation in the programs offered. I cannot even count the number of conversations I have had with faculty developers in my consulting role who are truly frustrated at the lack of engagement among their faculty. Yet, they share that faculty are the first to vent about the lack of or inadequacy of available support. Sure, there are those faculty members that will never engage or participate in career development programming, no matter how targeted or value add. I work with some of those faculty members who would greatly benefit but have no interest. While you might be able to persuade a few faculty who fall in this category to engage, my advice to you is do not spend too much time focused on these individuals. Instead, you are trying to find those faculty members who *are* interested in helping themselves; who seek the tools and guidance to continue their professional evolution as they aspire to find meaning in their careers.

In my work to date, I have found two factors contributing to a lack of engagement in available faculty development programming for a large portion of faculty, regardless of institution type: Communication and access. When I say communication, I am referring to a lack of clarity and consistency in terms of *who* communicates information about available programs, *how* program details are communicated, *where* resources and related information is available, and *how* engagement in faculty programming is facilitated (e.g., registration). You may recall the anecdote I shared in Chapter 3 about the faculty focus group I conducted. As a reminder, a focus group attendee shared her observations about the faculty development resources available on her campus, specifically her confusion about said resources and associated advancement processes based on what was communicated on an institutional webpage. Her peers had no idea the resources, or this web page, existed and were unsure of where to find it. She eventually did find it "by accident." This is an institutional-level problem.

By access I am referring to when programs are offered, the format of offerings (e.g., online, self-directed, small group workshop), and the target audience (e.g., career stage, division, women faculty, faculty of color). For example, a micro workshop on "Building a Course Syllabus" would appear to be aimed at an early career colleague who is just starting out in their career based on the workshop title. Yet, such a workshop could be very beneficial to a MCF member seeking to revise an existing course or re-envision a brand new course offering. Both of these populations of faculty members benefit from such a workshop, but it is not clear whom the target audience is not to mention the content of this workshop should differ based on audience and faculty member needs. The goal is to have a more strategic, targeted communication strategy to support your faculty development efforts. Further, you need to make sure that you are not inadvertently excluding key faculty members from engagement because you are not clear on the focus of the program, who you are targeting, or when you are offering that programming. In the following section, I present some important grounding on these two themes from the literature that can aid you as you continue to create the necessary infrastructure and communication strategy.

Organizational Communication

Effective communication in organizations does not happen without deliberateness and a focused strategy (Miller, 2008). A coherent communication strategy and infrastructure supports the flow of much-needed information related to institutional policies, health and safety concerns, important campus and community announcements, and campus events. According to the Society for Human Resource Management, "To be successful, organizations should have comprehensive policies and strategies for communicating with their constituencies, employees and stakeholders as well as with the community at large" (2017, para 1). An area that needs to be included in an institutional communication strategy is faculty development programming. Associated outcomes of effective organizational communication include increased employee morale and satisfaction (Bhatia & Balani, 2015; Shonubi et al., 2016); improved employee commitment and loyalty (Jiang & Men, 2017; Saad et al., 2018); organizational process and policy improvements (Bakotić & Krnić, 2016; Lewis, 2019); and reduced misunderstandings and increased clarity (Kim, 2018; Quirke, 2012).

According to the Society for Human Resource Management (2017), there are five core elements of an effective communication strategy: (1) effective strategies that engage senior leadership serving as models of top-down communication; (2) resources (e.g., a budget) that allow for the use of various forms of communication driven by intended message and audience; (3) a process that incorporates evaluation of a diversity of situations and the key messages that need to be shared about those situations; (4) methods for collecting and assessing feedback; and (5) the ability to customize message delivery facilitating concise and transparent communication. I return to these elements later in the chapter when discussing how Matt managed the challenges he faced at his institution.

Access

Supporting a robust portfolio of faculty development programming becomes nearly irrelevant if those programs are inaccessible to those who need it most or if those who are seeking to advance in their careers are unable to locate available resources. As you think about the faculty development programming on your campus, ask yourself the following questions. Are our faculty development programs offered on days and times that accommodate faculty members' professional and personal responsibilities? Do the formats of our offerings facilitate myriad ways to engage? Do we offer targeted faculty development programs (e.g., career stage, discipline, employment type) and are we clear about that focus in communications about programs offered? If the answer is "no" or "not as effectively as we could" you have now identified some key aspects that need to be accounted for in your communication strategy and execution plan.

Access is critically important to ensuring your faculty members are getting the support that they need *and* to realizing a return on your investment. I keep using the term faculty development portfolio because the goal should be offering robust programming that supports faculty members across all stages of the professoriate. As Werder (2018) so aptly noted, "Creating a career framework that starts with a specific job role and doesn't take it through a job family, career level, and career stream is like starting construction of a road and not completing it; it leads nowhere" (para 10). When situated in the context of the faculty career, this means supporting faculty as they advance from assistant, associate, and full professor. Learning and development does not stop once promotion and tenure are earned. Colleges and universities are missing out on developing the next generation of institutional leaders, community contributors, and life-long learners by failing to employ holistic career frameworks and instituting a clear, concise communication strategy to ensure those who need the information receive it.

I would be remiss if I did not highlight the relationship and present disconnects between access and faculty development programming for specific faculty populations, including women academics and faculty of color. Often conversations related to access require an examination of work-family or more recently career-friendly campus policies (Gerten, 2011). These issues are even more pronounced in a post-pandemic academy. Throughout the remainder of the chapter, I dive into these issues more explicitly as we return to Matt's challenges featured in the opening case. The subsequent actions featured in our discussion of tools, strategies, and resources outline the ways in which he improved communication and access in relation to his faculty development portfolio on his campus.

Returning to Matt's Experience

While there is always room for improvement and expansion when it comes to career development programming and related resources, there are fewer things more frustrating for campus leaders and administrators than a lack of engagement in program participation or feedback to support continuous program improvement. Yet, faculty still express displeasure at available resources and programming, or worse, it becomes clear they lack awareness about what is available to them. As faculty members who work with students, I think many of us can relate. We think we clearly explain the expectations on our syllabi, offer several ways to engage with course materials, and provide opportunities for input from students. Still, students lack understanding or need further explanation about where to get course-related resources when to us it is so obvious.

Matt is in a similar situation as he works to enhance existing faculty development offerings beyond early career and create the needed infrastructure to ensure key stakeholders are involved and faculty are aware of what is available to support their growth. As we dive into the opening case more deeply, I wonder if Matt's experience sounds familiar to you either as a campus leader charged with managing a career development program (office or center) on your campus. Alternatively, perhaps you are the faculty member who is unsure of what resources and programs are available on your campus that meet your needs, including career stage and discipline? In the space provided, write down some ideas and reactions to Matt's challenges and think about questions you would ask and suggestions you might offer him.

_____

_____

_____

_____

_____

_____

_____

_____

_____

_____

_____

_____

_____

_____

_____

_____

_____

_____

_____

_____

Relevant Facts

Based on the information provided, we know that Matt's institution has a fairly robust portfolio of faculty development programming, with increased investment in MCF programming over the past two-and-a-half years; a priority for Matt since assuming his director role. However, Matt's challenged by a lack of engagement in programs offered and a lack of feedback when requested from MCF as he works to enhance existing offerings.

Compounding this engagement problem is inadequate knowledge management systems at his institution that undergird effective faculty development. Matt lacks the data to track faculty along their trajectory. As a result, he is not as informed as he would like (and needs to be) in terms of time in rank (particularly for women and faculty of color), the efficacy of performance and evaluation processes, and overall satisfaction with the process for those faculty who have (and have not) been successful. This lack of knowledge makes it difficult to target communications to faculty populations most in need. This is an institutional improvement opportunity that Matt is poised to tackle with the right support from campus leadership.

Key Stakeholders

There are several implicit stakeholders that are important to Matt's situation. First, through his role he is focused on supporting faculty across their career journey at his institution. One of his driving priorities is to engage as many faculty as possible in programming and as faculty development co-creators, if you will, to provide much needed input into program offerings and faculty member needs.

Second, Matt must work closely with and articulate the return on investment to campus leaders and administrators. As shared throughout the book, faculty development is an investment in terms of time, finances, human capital, and infrastructure. It is not clear based on the information that is provided in the case if Matt was able to expand the faculty development portfolio through additional funding or a reallocation of funding. Regardless, he is required to share outcomes and impact of the center's programming and to illustrate a value add.

Third, there is an opportunity to coordinate with others involved in faculty development on Matt's campus. In fact, it appears this is an opportunity to enrich the efforts Matt is advancing by engaging in much needed capacity-building and to support the development of knowledge management systems. Remember—it takes a village to support faculty members.

Needed Information

I connected with Matt as someone who was gifted *Charting Your Path to Full* as a resource to include at his center. As he flipped through the pages, he found the Lead Mentor Development website and reached out. It was in his initial email that he shared much of what is noted in the opening case. From there, we scheduled a first meeting to talk through his needs. Prior to that first conversation, some issues arose for me and I drafted some corresponding questions. First, I did want to know more about his budget and how resource allocations were made that allowed room for MCF development programming. Second, I wanted to know more about how his success was defined and measured, specifically the metrics (e.g., number of programs offered yearly, faculty attendance, faculty satisfaction) used to assess his performance and to inform future resource allocations. Third, I needed to learn more about the types of faculty data he had access to and to talk through in more detail the types of data that would enable him to elevate the work he was doing through the Center.

I also felt it important to learn about how faculty development was supported more broadly at his institution. Referring back to Chapter 7, understanding who was responsible for faculty development and how that did or did not complement Matt's efforts was instrumental to crafting a plan moving forward. Lastly, I wanted to learn more about Matt's overall vision and career plan. How long did he plan to stay in this role, did he view his engagement as aligned with his own professional development plan, and how could we make sure his directorship was in service to his broader career plan?

Case Summary

Matt and the center have a great deal of potential to innovate and offer programming that is in service to faculty and to the institution. The goal becomes leveraging existing resources and creating the necessary infrastructure to effectively communicate programs and resources available. As part of our coaching relationship, Matt and I focused on building the infrastructure needed to increase the visibility of programs offered on his campus while also making it easy for faculty to find program resources. Matt knew he was missing an opportunity to engage a greater diversity of faculty members on his campus and the goal was to make it simple yet valuable for faculty to participate and benefit.

Tools, Strategies, and Resources

I return to the two critical considerations featured in the chapter to undergird our discussion of tools, resources, and strategies—communication and access. Your stakeholders need to know what support is available to them, and they need to be able to access those resources to support individual and institutional thriving. Drawing on best practices in organizational communication shared earlier, these practices are particularly salient when constructing a strategy to support effective communication and ensuring access to available faculty development programs and resources. It is these three practices that drove Matt's efforts to develop a strategy to support effective communication from his center to relevant stakeholders and to increase access to programs and resources.

Communication

First, it was important for Matt to have a clear process that enabled him and his staff to identify critical situations that require faculty development support either through focused training or access to resources, thus signaling the need for communication and other messaging. A recent example is the COVID-19 pandemic, particularly during the spring 2020 semester when faculty were required to switch to online teaching with little runway to do so. This situation made Matt realize his inability to adapt quickly and communicate in a timely, succinct manner to faculty across his campus was an issue.

Second, there needs to be various methods in which feedback can be gathered from targeted stakeholders that informs associated messaging and subsequent actions. Matt learned that email was not always the most effective means of communication either from his center or to it; his Center needed a central repository that helped filter faculty needs by themes or topic areas so he and his staff could more quickly and efficiently respond (and offer recommendations about which resources and programs would be most valuable).

Finally, the strategy must support customization of messaging for specific stakeholder groups and relevant to situations that may arise. Matt knew his early career colleagues, particularly those first or second year faculty were struggling during the pandemic, while his senior colleagues were challenged with changing pedagogies and needed training. Having data about different faculty populations and their needs would have helped him be more adept and reaching out to targeted groups of faculty to provide more tailored support.

Needed Infrastructure and Communication Strategies

Keeping the above learning lessons in mind, Matt and I tackled four areas as part of our time together: Faculty-driven knowledge management, "One-Stop Shopping" of available faculty related resources and programming, a focus on career-friendly policies and practices, and creating an inclusive faculty development community.

Faculty-Driven Knowledge Management. I first introduced the notion of Knowledge Management Systems in Chapter 5 as critical infrastructure that results in a high return on investment. As a reminder, a knowledge management system enables a department (or institution) to gather and organize collective knowledge and wisdom as well as track critical data about individuals, departments, and units on campus (Gurchiek, 2007). Such a system would enable Matt, for example, to get a better handle on the needs of faculty on his campus and to craft communications and messaging to targeted faculty populations who may be in need or struggling to advance along their intended career path.

The critical faculty data needed for Matt to more effectively engage in his role includes year of hire, a summary of yearly evaluation feedback (scanned/uploaded), summary interim/tenure review feedback (scanned/uploaded), and data about who is in formal leadership positions on campus (e.g., department or committee chair). This data would allow Matt to determine the pace at which a given faculty member is advancing along their career journey or to ensure faculty in formal leadership positions are receiving the training and tools they need to be successful. He can aggregate the data by gender and race, for example, to see if women and faculty of color are advancing at the same pace, or slower, compared to their white male peers. In addition, having a location in which faculty members can note goals, career aspirations, career stage and disciplinary needs, and leadership interests/experiences, would also be useful to Matt as he evaluates his faculty development portfolio and creates faculty population specific messaging. Such information would also support the identification and development of future campus leaders.

One-Stop Shopping. The majority of institutions and centers I have worked with have one foundational element in common—available faculty development resources, programming, and related communications emanate from across campus, making it confusing to determine who is responsible for what and where to go to in order to get the help and resources needed. The result is that no one takes full responsibility for oversight, and critical information is either unavailable or not communicated in a timely manner (or after the fact) to support the faculty members who need it most. I often joke that this results in The Wedding Singer response (a movie from the late 1990s starring Adam Sandler and Drew Barrymore); finding out about a program or resource that could have been helpful after it is too late elicits the "Could have been brought to my attention yesterday" response. The goal is to minimize these types of reactions from faculty across your campus.

Matt and I not only worked to streamline communications but we also created a central repository in which all related faculty development resources, programming, and entities were featured in one place to allow for "One-Stop-Shopping." Creating this resource was a campus-wide effort and required setting aside egos about who was responsible for which aspect and who should get credit. Instead, the focus was on the value add and usability of the end user—faculty members. A campus-wide webpage called "Faculty Programming and Resources" was created and included all relevant URLs to other campus webpages. The Faculty Programming and Resources URL was added to all contributing offices, units, and committees webpages.

The Faculty Programming and Resources page was organized to include:

- Faculty development training and workshops (e.g., campus calendar with related events, workshop descriptions, registration links)
- Available resources (e.g., faculty development funds with instructions on how to apply, relevant offices along with the point of contact name, email, and phone number)
- Request support (e.g., sign up for formal mentoring, ask to observe teaching/request to have someone observe your teaching, request a one-on-one coaching session)
- Share your success (e.g., provided space for faculty to upload details about recent conference presentations, publications, teaching successes).

Matt and I focused on ensuring that engagement, either as a participant or as a contributor, was so simple that one would feel almost embarrassed to admit they have been disengaged. Further, two critical aims were accomplished by investing in faculty-specific knowledge management systems and in creating "One-Stop-Shopping." First, Matt's programming investments and other related decisions were informed and driven by robust data that could be aggregated, allowing him to tailor programming and messaging to specific faculty populations most in need. He literally started sending personalized emails to faculty members who were at the associate professor rank to schedule meetings, learn about their career plans, and explain his center might be able to assist in their efforts to advance to full. Second, he was able to begin changing the culture related to faculty development by making engagement so easy that everyone viewed the Faculty Programming and Resources page as *the* place to go for help.

In the space provided, write down your thoughts about what Matt implemented at his institution. Do you already engage in some of these actions? Collect this type of data? Do you have a central resource that makes it easy for faculty to find what they need in one space? If you answer "yes," good for you! Keep it up. If the answer is "no" or "not as comprehensively as we could be doing," write down a plan below (e.g., who to speak with, what offices/individuals need to be involved).

Access

Now that you have the data in hand (or at least know what data you should have) about faculty needs and all related resources are organized in one central website, the next hurdle to tackle is access. Most campus leaders and those tasked with faculty development responsibilities believe their programs and resources are fully accessible to those who need it most. But, when pressed on this point further, cracks start to surface—perhaps offering that program on the weekend is not as accessible as you thought or the after-work sessions you schedule to avoid class time conflicts is not as workable as you imagined. The goal is about reviewing and revising policies and programming to be more career friendly (note I do not say work-family friendly) and to create a more inclusive faculty development community.

Career-Friendly. As Matt and I began to dive into the topic of access, I asked him one simple question—Are the intended faculty populations and/or the faculty who most need support, able to take advantage of the programs and resources offered? Matt thought about this question for a minute or two and realized, he could not fully answer that question because he was not sure, despite believing that they could. As we dove deeper into the data he did already have in hand, he found that few women and faculty of color participated in their leadership development offerings mostly offered in the evenings and weekends. Matt also found that MCF were not participating in teaching-related programs to the level he thought they would given their institutional context is a community college. These trends alarmed him and perplexed him.

Matt's institution has implemented several work-family policies on campus, which research shows provides needed awareness about related career challenges and supports for women faculty and graduate students pursuing a career in the academy (Beddoes & Pawley, 2014). Further, research by Pedulla and Thébaud (2015) revealed "Although supportive, work-family policies alone may not be sufficient to reshape gender inequality in the worlds of work and relationships, our findings indicate that institutional environments and policies matter" (p. 134).

While work-family policies are and continue to be important, scholars have refocused the conversation on the need for separate career-friendly policies from family-friendly policies "to tackle persistent gender inequity for this subgroup of women academics" (Gerten, 2011, p. 47). Despite the presence of work-family policies such as "stop the clock" which allows faculty, particularly women, to postpone going up for tenure and promotion, there is pressure to not take advantage of these policies given the negative career consequences that follow such as increased pay inequities and stalled career advancement (Bourdeau et al., 2019; Gerten, 2011). Matt and I thought through the implications of this on faculty development and type of support he provided. He realized he needed to get creative in how programs and related resources were made available and delivered to women faculty, particularly academic mothers, and faculty of color who carry a disproportionate service load at the institution.

Matt focused on adjusting timing of offerings, format of offerings (online, self-paced, accessible 24 hours a day), and increasing resources available (e.g., rubrics, career development, templates) to support faculty. Matt also offered more one-on-one coaching sessions through the center either by himself or other faculty subject matter experts across his campus (who received a modest honorarium for their time commitment). Note once Matt assumed this position, his role is mostly focused on this administrative post, teaching only one or two courses per year. He also created more in-person workshops that were population specific (e.g., career stage, women faculty, faculty of color) to help reduce power differentials and to create sub-communities around collective experiences.

Inclusive Faculty Development Community. As we think about creating a more inclusive faculty development community on our respective campuses, I turn to the work of my friends and colleagues Drs. Leslie Gonzales (Michigan State University) and Kimberly Griffin (University of Maryland) who are serving as co-leads of the Aspire Alliance Research Team, a multi-institutional alliance supported by the National Science Foundation. As part of their collective work, they co-authored a report titled, "Supporting faculty during and after COVID-19: Don't let go of equity," in which they outlined the predominant ways institutions were responding to COVID-19 in relation to faculty support and evaluation. Many of the themes featured in their report have been discussed throughout this book, such as creating extension policies, recognizing a dip in faculty productivity, and accounting for emotional (invisible) labor—all issues that predominantly effect women faculty and faculty of color disproportionately.

As Gonzales and Griffin (2020) so aptly noted, "Looking ahead, decision makers must anticipate the kinds of support that faculty may need as they continue to manage the personal and professional implications of COVID-19. Like evaluative processes, support systems require attention to equity" (p. 7). They offer four foundational elements: Efforts moving forward must include diverse stakeholders spanning campus leaders, committees, faculty developers and faculty members; acknowledgement must be made regarding how the academy is different pre- and post-pandemic and faculty support must adapt as a result; emotional and invisible labor is real and must be made visible in evaluation of faculty work; and instructional technologists need to be members of the core faculty development team. I strongly encourage you to read the report and review the additional faculty development resources offered as you seek to create a more inclusive faculty development community.

In summary, the outcomes of focusing on communication and access are twofold. First, the resources and strategies noted here can (and will) inform your organizational communication strategy thus increasing engagement in faculty development programming on your campus. Second, by working to increase and facilitate access, you are creating a culture of growth and development, one grounded in career-friendly practices. Further, you will be able to highlight the great work of faculty in the areas of teaching, scholarship, and service as you foster an inclusive faculty development community.

Chapter Summary and Next Steps

Faculty developers and institutional leaders invest a great deal of time and resources into supporting faculty members, specifically in terms of career development programming. Fewer things are more professionally frustrating than providing support—support that you know is wanted (and needed)—and yet the engagement is not at the level you expect. You scratch your head trying to figure out why this is happening. You then realize—**Existing institutional infrastructure does not highlight or promote faculty development programming**—the featured problem in this chapter.

The focus of this chapter is on two critical considerations that should undergird all faculty development efforts: Communication and access. If you do not create the needed communication strategy and associated infrastructure to keep your faculty members informed about what is available, when, and in what ways they can participate, you will continue to see lower than expected faculty engagement. Your supports and programming must be accessible, otherwise you will continue to be disappointed and so will your faculty. As we traverse a post-pandemic academy, it is time to think about strategic investments, such as knowledge management systems and engaging key campus constituents in reviews of current faculty advancement and development processes as we work to create a more inclusive faculty development culture and community on our campuses. Related suggestions were offered throughout, relying on Matt's experiences to illustrate how these tools, resources, and strategies could be implemented.

As we look ahead to the concluding chapter of the book (Chapter 9), I want you to think about the knowledge gleaned and critical lessons learned throughout this book. Most certainly you realized you are further along than you realized; I am sure you also identified opportunities for improvement at the individual, departmental, and institutional levels. A common practice I employ when conducting workshops or keynote addresses is incorporating a "call to action" to ensure you walk away from our time together with explicit actions to advance your work and professional agenda. Be thinking about what that might look like for you.

References

Bakotić, D and Krnić, A. (2016). Exploring the relationship between business process improvement and employees' behavior. *Journal of Organizational Change Management*, 30(7), 1044–1062. https://doi.org/10.1108/JOCM-06-2016-0116

Beddoes, K., & Pawley, A. L. (2014). "Different people have different priorities": Work–family balance, gender, and the discourse of choice. *Studies in Higher Education*, 39(9), 1573–1585.

Bhatia, K., & Balani, M. (2015, November). Effective internal communication: A crucial factor affecting employee performance. In *Proceedings of international conference on management, economics and social sciences, Dubai* (pp. 135–142).

Bourdeau, S., Ollier-Malaterre, A., & Houlfort, N. (2019). Not all work-life policies are created equal: Career consequences of using enabling versus enclosing work-life policies. *Academy of Management Review*, 44(1), 172–193.

Gerten, A. M. (2011). Moving beyond family-friendly policies for faculty mothers. *Affilia*, 26(1), 47–58.

Gonzales, L., & Griffin, K. A (2020). Supporting faculty during and after COVID-19. *Aspire: The National Alliance for Inclusive and Diverse STEM Faculty*. https://drive.google.com/file/d/1WQrIG6LsR04jGASfF6Z8WVxl4RI RpsMj/view

Gurchiek, K. (2007, October 1). Few organizations have plans to stem brain drain. *SHRM*. www.shrm.org/hr-today/news/hr-news/pages/cms_023170.aspx

Jiang, H., & Men, R. L. (2017). Creating an engaged workforce: The impact of authentic leadership, transparent organizational communication, and work-life enrichment. *Communication Research*, 44(2), 225–243.

Kim, Y. (2018). Enhancing employee communication behaviors for sensemaking and sensegiving in crisis situations: Strategic management approach for effective internal crisis communication. *Journal of Communication Management*, 22(4), 451–475. doi:10.1108/JCOM-03-2018-0025

Lewis, L. (2019). Organizational change. In A. M. Nicotera (Ed.), *Origins and traditions of organizational communication* (pp. 406–423). Routledge.

Miller, K. (2008). *Organizational communication: Approaches and processes* (4th ed.). Wadsworth/Thomson Learning.

Pedulla, D. S., & Thébaud, S. (2015). Can we finish the revolution? Gender, work-family ideals, and institutional constraint. *American Sociological Review*, 80(1), 116–139.

Quirke, M. B. (2012). *Making the connections: Using internal communication to turn strategy into action*. Gower Publishing, Ltd.

Saad, Z. M., Sudin, S., & Shamsuddin, N. (2018). The influence of leadership style, personality attributes and employee communication on employee engagement. *Global Business and Management Research*, 10(3), 743.

Shonubi, O. A., Abdullah, N., Hashim, R., & Ab Hamid, N. (2016). Psychological influence of organizational communication on employee job satisfaction and organizational commitment: a review. *Journal of Human Capital Development (JHCD)*, *9*(1), 85–94.

Society for Human Resource Management (2017). Managing organizational communication. *SHRM Toolkits*. www.shrm.org/resourcesandtools/tools-and-samples/toolkits/pages/managingorganizationalcommunication.aspx

Werder, C. (2018, August 30). 5 career development essentials. *Training*. https://trainingmag.com/5-career-development-essentials/

Part 3

Thriving at Mid-Career

Chapter 9

Moving Forward
A Mid-Career Agenda

Mid-career is a unique time in work and life. Opportunities for growth, learning, and continued development abound. However, in order to capitalize on such opportunities, one needs guidance, resources, and support. I write this book as a mid-career scholar—one seeking opportunities to continue to grow and develop. I also write this book as someone with a formal leadership position on my campus that affords me opportunities to work with students and faculty alike, contributing to their professional evolution. I write this book as someone who has the great fortune to work with faculty and campus leaders from all institution types around the globe on the topics of faculty and leadership development. Finally, I write this book as a mother and wife, two roles that are of utmost importance, which influence the opportunities I pursue (and the ones I pass on). It is these identities and experiences that motivated me to share my expertise as broadly as possible to assist all members of the academy as they seek to re-envision mid-career and manage this moment in their work and personal lives.

I recently served as a faculty speaker for the Academic Leadership Academy (ALA) hosted by Penn State University's Center for the Study of Higher Education. Fifty academic leaders attended, focused on building their own competencies while enhancing their leadership toolkits and network. I facilitated workshops focused on career advancement; specifically I walked attendees through the steps to assess one's existing career advancement portfolio (Chapter 7) as well as how to enhance career advancement supports on their respective campuses. My aim was to equip them with tools and resources that they could use to manage career advancement for their team members as well as their own career advancement. We then reconvened six weeks later to determine the academic leaders' progress as they continued to develop career advancement processes and programs on their own campuses.

During the first breakout session, attendees discussed the challenges present in their career advancement plans and processes (current and

DOI: 10.4324/9781003201311-13

aspirational). The usual suspects surfaced such as limited time, resources, and personnel to manage the career advancement plans present on their respective campuses. Other issues such as lack of value ascribed to comprehensive career advancement processes as evidenced by resource cuts and poor campus culture were also noted. While attendees spoke genuinely about their desire to support the career advancement of their team members, as well as their own, they lamented the lack of knowledge they have or support available to increase their knowledge.

While insights gleaned from the ALA participants informed knowledge shared in this final chapter, I return to the experiences of the individuals featured in each chapter to restate the featured problem and summarize the main contributions of each chapter. I then highlight four opportunities we can all pursue in terms of career advancement on our respective campuses.

Chapter Summaries

Earning P&T, in a system in which tenure exists, is the proverbial brass ring that academics work toward when they embark on their path to the professoriate. There are dedicated resources such as formal mentoring programs, regular performance reviews, and national efforts targeted toward early career colleagues to help them advance along the early years of their careers. Such support is paramount to attracting and retaining a diverse faculty body across all institution types in higher education. However, the support that accompanies the early career stage is either greatly diminished or nonexistent once that hurdle is surpassed. To combat the reduced support, mid-career faculty (MCF) need guidance and resources to help them navigate their careers, whether they are new to the mid-career club or are a seasoned veteran. Articulating career advancement goals, developing plans to achieve those goals, engaging your network of mentors, and crafting and implementing an execution strategy is critical to ensure success. This foundation is particularly important for women and faculty of color given the immense amount of invisible labor they engage in as they support our students and our institutions (Matthew, 2016).

Part 1—Individual Faculty Perspective

Part 1 of this book shined a light on the individual faculty perspective, specifically the challenges, needs, and opportunities for MCF. Organized around critical problems that surface during mid-career, Chapters 1–4 provide MCF with a scaffolded approach to advancing along their career as they work toward career goals, such as earning full professorship, securing a senior leadership position, or seeking fulfillment and engagement in their career.

In Chapter 1 you were introduced to Sam, an associate professor in STEM at a comprehensive university. He had aspirations of earning full professorship but quickly realized the **lack of clearly defined career hurdles and developmental milestones** was problematic, making it challenging to envision his path forward. While the mid-career stage is long and ill-defined, it can also be a time for personal and professional growth, risk-taking, and re-invention. As faculty evolve in their careers, they need tools, strategies, and resources to help them engage in a self-assessment that puts them on a path to achieving their career goals. Guided reflections such as "Fly on the Wall" and "Key Contributions," as well as performance feedback tools such as the Modified 360-degree Assessment equip MCF with the knowledge and data needed to establish career goals. Sam was able to use these tools to help him gain a better handle on his professional status to begin envisioning next steps to achieve his full professorship goal.

Chapter 2 tackles the problem of **limited dedicated resources and developmental programming aimed at mid-career,** an issue that permeates the academy regardless of institution type and geography. If you recall Sarah, the associate professor in the humanities at a liberal arts college, deliberately chose not to pursue full professorship after earning promotion and tenure given her personal roles as wife and mother to two young children. Once her kids entered elementary school, she began reconsidering advancement to full, but felt she was pursuing this goal somewhat blindly. Higher education is changing, and that change has been accelerated by the COVID-19 pandemic. Rather than work toward a "return to normal" in the academy, the aim should be to re-evaluate needed supports for MCF that better align with the realities and face of the academy moving forward. Sarah worked through the various activities and tools presented in this chapter including the post hoc "Year in Review," Strategic Professional Planning, and Problem Solving tactics. The aim—help you clearly articulate your career goals and map out plans to achieve those goals, which were just the jump starter that Sarah needed.

After working your way through the tools, strategies and resources in Chapters 1 and 2, you have a better handle on your performance given you have engaged a diversity of individuals to offer you feedback. You identified your career goals, mapped out plans to achieve those goals, and established some strategies to tackle problems that arise throughout your career advancement path. Nevertheless, you still need support to manage the featured problem in Chapter 3, **inadequate guidance on how to advance toward professional (and personal) goals.** You may have found yourself identifying with Ashley, our faculty peer in the fine and applied arts at a research university. She aspired to earn full professorship and was in the midst of navigating that process at her institution. She was unclear about the process and who was responsible for executing the different aspects. To help overcome this issue, this chapter provided specific direction on where to locate institutional information about promotion and advancement criteria and processes and taught you how to leverage faculty handbook language and institutional strategic imperatives to frame your dossier or other advancement aspirations. Through the use of a career progression framework you mapped out specific goals, created timelines for completion, and connected your goals and related engagement to institutional priorities and imperatives. Your career progression framework serves as a visual tool of your career plans and helps you hold yourself accountable.

Congratulations, you have done the hard work to get to the point of having clearly articulated career goals and a path to achieve those goals. Yet, maybe you have fallen short in achieving your goals, or perhaps you are failing to achieve your goals in the desired (or needed) timeframe. You may recall this happened to Brad, our STEM colleague employed at a regional comprehensive university featured in the opening case in Chapter 4. He had plans to achieve full professorship and earn a deanship at his institution, yet the execution of his plans was lacking; he needed to reassess and re-envision. Maybe you are trying to be proactive to avoid the trap that Brad and so many others fall in—knowing what to do, but failing to follow through. Regardless of your situation, Chapter 4 really targets this issue by addressing the featured problem of **no formal strategy and/or poorly articulated advancement plans.** The aim of this chapter is to provide you with the needed grounding to execute your plans effectively. A detailed five-step strategy execution process is offered along with a Scenario Planning Strategy Framework to really guide your efforts. You saw the framework in action using Brad's career goals and aims as the foundation. In this chapter, you created a process that allows for your goals and plans to evolve, engages critical stakeholders and mentors in the process, and monitors your progress to ensure success.

Your career advancement is your responsibility. However, that does not mean you are no longer in need of mentoring and guidance as you continue to advance along your career. Part 1 of the book is meant to provide you with that guidance; to serve as the "pocket mentor" we all need as we traverse our career advancement journey. Come back to these tools, strategies, and resources at various points along your path. You will continue to evolve. Be sure to honor that evolution by giving yourself the time and space to engage in the reflection, work, and thinking needed to feel fulfilled.

Part 2—Departmental and Institutional Perspectives

While Part 1 of the book focused on the individual faculty perspective and career advancement processes, Part 2 hones in on offering guidance in service to specific leadership positions (e.g., department chair) and institutional perspectives. As campus leaders and faculty developers seek to support and assess a robust portfolio of faculty and career development programming and resources, they too need mentorship and guidance to achieve desired programmatic results and foster their own professional growth. Chapters 5 through 8 provide that needed guidance.

We were introduced to Natalie, a social scientist and first-time department chair at a liberal arts college in Chapter 5. Despite having a wonderful role model and advocate in her previous department chair, Natalie was deeply concerned about the lack of institutional support or training offered on her campus, a concern shared by the two fellow newly appointed department chairs on her campus. Natalie's experiences highlighted the featured problem for those tasked with leadership responsibilities on their respective campus, which is a **disconnect between role expectations and available training and development to achieve expectations**. For those assuming leadership responsibilities, there is a new triumvirate you must manage: Leadership, management, and personnel development (as well as your own career growth and advancement). This chapter helped you identify and gain the knowledge needed to be effective as a department chair. Additionally, specific strategies were offered on how to enhance your toolkit of personnel development approaches by highlighting the utility of developmental career advancement appraisals. Given the lack of formal leadership training across the academy, Chapter 5 established the groundwork for you to take control over your own leadership development and to help those who follow in your footsteps.

Chapter 6 continued the focus on the department chair role and made the case for mentorship for leaders. Adam, a second-term department chair in the fine and applied arts at a community college, finally felt like he was hitting his stride when concerns about his own career advancement surfaced. After he engaged in a self-assessment of his prospects for full professorship, he realized his own creative productivity greatly reduced; he felt like he needed to start over, and that was a daunting task. Adam is not alone in this feeling. In fact, many department chairs struggle with managing their administrative and leadership responsibilities while pursuing their own professional pursuits. This reality is the basis for the featured problem in Chapter 6, which is **limited access to mentors to support your career advancement while serving as department chair**. Simply stated, leaders need mentoring too and this chapter focused on how mentorships need to evolve given the realities of the mid-career stage. Adam was able to work through the mentoring needs inventory as he sought to build his own team of supporters. Finally, this chapter offered guidance on how to use delegation to both manage your responsibilities as department chair and to create a departmental culture of accountability.

Chapter 7 offered an institutional-level perspective by introducing you to Francis, a full professor and dean of faculty at a research university. Despite being a full professor, Francis is very much in the mid-career stage, and it was her own experiences as a faculty member working to manage the rigors of mid-career that motivated her to pursue this leadership position. Her goal is to enhance her existing portfolio of faculty development programming with a focused eye on increasing her budget to broaden supports for MCF. Her aim fully illustrates the featured institutional-level problem featured in Chapter 7: **Existing faculty development programming does not meet the needs of seasoned faculty or the institutions that employ them.** While faculty members have responsibility for managing their careers, I am a firm believer that institutions have a responsibility to provide the needed resources to ensure faculty can "meet expectations" and manage their careers effectively. Chapter 7 walked you through the steps of a faculty development portfolio assessment requiring you to have clarity about who or what has faculty development responsibility on your campus. Additionally, the assessment encouraged a thorough accounting of the programs and resources available to faculty and asked you to clearly state the performance expectations. You cannot expect faculty to perform across the areas noted in your faculty handbook if you do not provide resources, tools, and support that align with those performance areas. The knowledge gleaned from this assessment is vital to ensuring your portfolio of supports meet individual and institutional needs.

In Chapter 8, the final content chapter of this book, we met Matt who is a full professor in STEM and the Director of the Center for Faculty Development at a community college. Despite the center's limited resources, Matt felt grateful for the robust portfolio of faculty development supports and related programming available to his colleagues across campus. Yet, he grew frustrated by a lack of faculty engagement in terms of attendance and feedback from the faculty members he served. Matt also acknowledges the need for improved knowledge management systems at his disposal to better meet the needs of specific populations of faculty on his campus, specifically women and faculty of color. Matt's frustration illustrates that **existing institutional infrastructure does not highlight or promote faculty development programming,** the featured problem in Chapter 8. This chapter highlighted two foundational issues that must be accounted for to ensure you have a robust portfolio of faculty development supports *and* those supports are serving your faculty to the fullest extent possible—communication and access. Chapter 8 included the need for a strategic communication strategy that incorporates faculty-driven knowledge management systems, one-stop-shopping of faculty development resources, career-friendly policies and practices, and actions for creating an inclusive faculty development community.

Re-writing the Mid-Career Narrative: Advancing an Institutional and Faculty-Focused Agenda

As I think about the future of mid-career across the academy and the ways in which we can better support our mid-career colleagues and institutions, I return to the academic leaders I had the great fortunate of working with through Penn State University's ALA. As we concluded our first working session together, I hosted a second small group breakout in which I asked attendees to think about and record the career advancement opportunities on their campuses. I was struck by their responses. The opportunities they shared continue to inspire and motivate me to pursue a career helping others advance in theirs. In the following section, I highlight four opportunities to inform and propel related efforts on your campus.

Equity Mindedness

Almost all of the small group discussions highlighted equity mindedness as an opportunity on their respective campuses and the academy more broadly. In fact, I will go as far to say that all career advancement policies, practices, and supports must, at their core, be built, implemented, and assessed from an equity mindset. For far too long this has not been the reality, and the implications of that are real, pervasive, and detrimental, particularly for women and faculty of color colleagues (Corley, 2020).

Willis (2020a) brilliantly lays out thoughtful and accessible actions we all can take to move forward career advancement work on our own campuses informed by an equity lens. Her first action step focuses on the need to be educated about equity on your own campus and to identify the equity issues most salient to you. The goal is to be an advocate and ensure equity is a driver of related career advancement efforts. There are a wealth of related resources available, as well as subject matter experts who can provide guidance and coaching on issues of equity.

While challenging, and perhaps unflattering, the process of educating yourself also requires personal self-reflection about the ways in which you may be contributing to inequities on your campus, in your department, and in your classroom. For many of us, including myself, this means acknowledging my own privilege as I seek to serve as an advocate and voice for advancing equity mindedness on my campus. This also requires seeking guidance, resources, and support outside of your own campus, to leverage your networks, and to ask the hard questions of others as you strive to evolve and contribute to equity mindedness in meaningful ways. The aim is to expose oneself to other perspectives and to examine our own biases and assumptions as we intentionally seek to listen and learn.

Willis (2020a) ends her recommendations by noting the importance of teaching others and yielding to marginalized voices. As Willis states, "Another important Y is, say yes to a sustained commitment. When the dust has settled and the protests have stopped, will you continue to promote equity?" (para 21). I found this to be a powerful question and a reminder that equity-minded work is a process, not a final destination and we must ground our career advancement work in an equity lens if we are to attract, retain, and support a diversity of talented faculty (and staff) across the academy.

Strategic Partnerships

In a post-pandemic higher education landscape, perhaps now more than ever strategic partnerships are needed to drive career advancement work forward. I urge you to think beyond the traditional partners such as the center for teaching and learning, the center for faculty development, and human resources. Of course, these are vital and must continue to factor into your network of partnerships prominently, but you must think beyond the obvious choices.

In the present-day academy, your strategic partnerships must include offices and individuals with diversity, equity, and inclusion expertise and related programming. If you do not have anyone or any department or unit with this expertise on your campus, look outside of your institution. Willis (2020b) writes compellingly on this topic from the perspective of a job seeker as she offers advice to ascertain which institutions are truly committed and invested in doing diversity, equity, and inclusion work as a differentiator. Remember, inauthenticity at the institutional and individual levels is obvious. You must put in the work knowing it requires an ongoing commitment.

Consider various consortia with which you and your institution have or seek membership. Think creatively and innovatively about how you might pool resources and facilitate cross-institutional networks and communities to complement and enhance your career advancement programming and related resources. It is also worthwhile to find institutions, whether a member of your consortia or not, engaged in innovative and effective career advancement work. Schedule time to meet with the key architects of these efforts to figure out if there are possibilities to share resources.

Find professional associations and networks in which there is shared community and commitment to supporting learning and professional advancement. In STEM, for example, there are a variety of organization focused change networks (Austin et al., 2019), such as the Center for the Integration of Research, Teaching, and Learning and the Network of STEM Education Centers, which brings together a group of likeminded professionals focused on advancing STEM reform initiatives. These communities provide resources, tools, and professional development opportunities for members to leverage and bring back to their home campuses.

Re-defining Success

Advancing along one's career path requires clarity about how success is defined and measured. My time with the ALA attendees focused a great deal on the importance of defining success for various institutional roles and revisiting that definition to adapt as needed. Additionally, explicit efforts must be outlined in terms of how success is measured. Guiding questions include asking yourself: What are the key performance indicators (KPIs) for faculty or staff on your respective campus? How are those KPIs collected/measured? How is knowledge gleaned from assessment efforts used to make needed change and support the career advancement of the incumbent? I fail to see how we, as members of the academy, can hold ourselves and others accountable *and* provide the needed supports to achieve success, if we fail to be explicit about how success is defined, measured, and assessed.

What I hope surfaced for you is the need to shift how success is defined, measured, and assessed in a post-pandemic academy. Conversations amongst ALA attendees arose about how to make the invisible work of women academics, BIPOC, and LGBTQIA faculty visible and relevant to re-defining success, for example. In addition, success should vary for different populations of faculty, accounting for career stage, discipline, and appointment type. What are institutions doing to actively ensure their faculty, regardless of appointment type and career stage, are meeting agreed upon expectations for performance?

Related, we had conversations about the need to change the narrative, particularly the language around performance expectations and the term itself. What if we replaced the word "performance" with "advancement"? This shift is simple yet powerful. It acknowledges the professional growth and evolution that individuals experience along their career trajectory. Success and associated KPIs look quite different in a career advancement model given the term, by its very nature, accounts for constant growth. Performance conversely signals a more finite event, creating an either/or (e.g., you performed at expected levels/you did not perform at expected levels) scenario, which fosters a deficit, rather than growth mindset (Ackerman, 2021; Dweck, 2016).

Support Non-Standard Career Advancement

Finally, career advancement needs to account for non-standard or non-traditional career paths. As highlighted earlier in this book, reliance on non-tenure track and adjunct faculty is on the rise across all institution types. We rely on these individuals to contribute in meaningful ways to our students, departments, and institutions. Yet, they are not always afforded access to the same types of career advancement resources and programming provided to tenure track and tenured faculty. Many mid-career professionals are among this population of faculty also dealing with the rigors that accompany life and work during the mid-career season. Failing to provide access to resources, programming, and mentoring to this population of faculty is nothing short of a disservice to the individual and the institution.

I also want to highlight the mid-career professional who straddles administrative and faculty roles either as tenure track or as tenured members of the academy or through courtesy teaching appointments. Performance expectations differ across these two roles, as do the career advancement opportunities, and rarely do these roles intersect but rather operate in parallel. The administrative side requires training and development in leadership, management, and personnel development (see Chapter 5); the faculty or teaching role requires teaching and learning support, resources in assessment and course development, and knowledge of student services across campus. I have interacted with many faculty who appreciate the diversity such an appointment affords; however, such appointments also come at a cost as one foot is firmly planted in different roles, as the individual works to be fully effective when their appointment is only part-time in either position. The reality is the incumbent is working two full time jobs, despite what their appointment letter states.

Lastly, we need to constantly remind ourselves that leadership happens in a variety of contexts outside the confines of formal, traditional leadership roles on our respective campuses. Leadership development must account for this reality. A faculty colleague may not aspire to serve as department chair, for example, but would certainly benefit from having access to and participation in training and development focused on delegation, vision setting, and interpersonal communication, for example. Further, understanding how higher education budgets work and how data-informed decisions are made across the academy is pertinent knowledge we all need to understand. We have faculty leaders in our classrooms, in scholarship and creative inquiry, in our communities, and in professional associations. We need to acknowledge, encourage, and support formal and informal leaders across the academy.

Concluding Thoughts

Not a day goes by where I do not feel a deep sense of gratitude for the privilege of pursuing a career in higher education. During my career to date, I have met some incredible human beings who have pushed me to be my best and who have contributed in meaningful ways to my own career growth and progression. I also know I am better because of those individuals, and I aspire to help elevate the performance and behaviors of those around me. In order to do that, however, we must provide individuals with the tools, resources, and strategies to rise to the occasion so we, as members of the academy, can benefit from their knowledge, their lived experiences, and their creativity and innovation. I write this book to shed light on the needs and opportunities of faculty, department chairs, and institutional leaders. My sincere hope is this book serves as a springboard for you and your institution to achieve greatness as you seek to advance along your career journey and as you support those you are tasked with supporting along theirs.

References

Ackerman, C. E. (2021, May 31). Growth mindset vs fixed + key takeaways from Dweck's book. *Positive Psychology.* https://positivepsychology.com/growth-mindset-vs-fixed-mindset/

Austin, A. E., Singer, S., Baker, V. L., Bae, S., Grimm, A., Ring, M., Shanks, L., Starck, S., & Storer, A. (2019, May). Organizational change networks (OCN): Drivers of change in undergraduate STEM education. Poster session presented at the annual meeting of the Network of STEM Education Centers, Omaha, NE.

Corley, J. (2020, June 27). Where are the women of color in academia? *Forbes.* www.forbes.com/sites/jacquelyncorley/2020/06/27/where-are-the-women-of-color-in-academia/?sh=29a067e36401

Dweck, C. (2016). What having a "growth mindset" actually means. *Harvard Business Review, 13,* 213–226.

Matthew, P. A. (2016). What is faculty diversity worth to a university. *The Atlantic.* www.theatlantic.com/education/archive/2016/11/what-is-faculty-diversity-worth-to-a-university/508334/

Willis, D. S. (2020a, June 22). Career exploration through the lends of equity. *Inside HigherEd.* www.insidehighered.com/advice/2020/06/22/some-practical-strategies-becoming-more-equity-minded-scholar-opinion

Willis, D. S. (2020b, December 14). Job seeker, change agent. *Inside HigherEd.* www.insidehighered.com/advice/2020/12/14/how-be-change-agent-diversity-equity-and-inclusion-your-career-and-job-search

Index

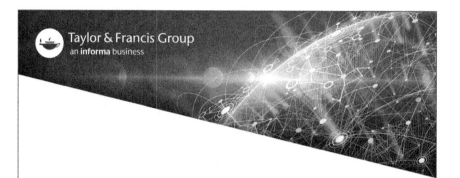

Printed in the United States
by Baker & Taylor Publisher Services